POIKILOPAIDIA

Poems
(1960-2020)

Peter Gimpel

RHP

POIKILOPAIDIA; Poems (1960 – 2020), by Peter Gimpel
Copyright © 2022 by Peter C. Gimpel
First Edition

Published in the United States by Red Heifer Press
410 Oakwood Court
Tehachapi, California 93561
All rights reserved.

Cover Design by Red Heifer Press
Typesetting and book design by Red Heifer Press.

ISBN: 978-0-9855199-4-0

Acknowledgments & Dedication

The publishing of this collection of poems was made possible through the generosity of some very dear friends (listed in alphabetical order).

Daniel Chodos
Susan Minor
Jim and Yun Murphy
Yu-Ting Peng
Harriet Zeitlin
Jan Zeitlin

Their support was given without knowledge of the contents of this collection, and was not an endorsement of any of the views, opinions or ideas expressed herein.

Several of the poems dated from 2012 forward were first tried in Open Mic at Tehachapi's Fiddlers Crossing, the internationally noted folk-music venue run by Peter Cutler and Deborah Hand. I thank them warmly, and also the Tehachapi Poets Society, our local group of stationary minstrels.

I cannot fail to mention, over his vehement objection, Stamatis Philippides of the University of Crete, a dear and valued friend for more than 40 years, who provided invaluable criticism, stimulus, and materials for many of my poems, translations, and ideas.

My uncle Bronislaw Gimpel paid for my first venture into print in 1976. After a cellist friend and I played the Saint-Saens concerto for him in 1965, my uncle asked me to tour with him as his accompanist. Knowing my limitations as a pianist and musician, I declined. I have never forgotten his loving friendship and unfailing support. One of the great violin virtuosi of the 20th Century, he was a charming and unassuming man. In his hands, the violin didn't just sing; it spoke, it reasoned, it growled, it pleaded, whispered, burned, raged, glowed, made love, and raised its voice to Heaven, along with anyone who listened. It is to his memory that I humbly dedicate this volume.

P.G.

Foreword

My early approaches to American poets and poetry editors were greeted with such withering condescension that I recoiled from publishing altogether. I stopped submitting my poems to journals when I realized that the literary sherpas were radically against my way of writing, thinking, feeling; indeed, downright opposed to the classical tradition—as if they had studied it and understood it (which they hadn't), and judged it synonymous with sterile imitation and literary and social irrelevance (which they had).

Thus, except for a few readings and some gratifying reviews in the Jewish press of my selected poems (*Twilight with Halfmoon Rising*) and my polymorphic novel (*The Carnevalis of Eusebius Asch*), my work has progressed largely unnoticed. Nor did I have time to hawk my wares, as an author is condemned to do for the rest of his life, according to an old Yiddish saying.

I did continue writing, however, because it pleased me to believe that I was good at it, and that I was saying some things that needed to be said that other writers were not saying; and because a few people whose judgement I respected agreed with me. Indeed, at some point I began to imagine that a duty had devolved on me to make a record of my untypical experience as a sentient being, a Jew, and an American. Looking over my collected poems, correcting and revising them, I think I have assembled such a record, though perhaps not as good or complete a one as I might have wished. It does, however, offer an unusual perspective, and one that I still believe is valid.

Had my life been simpler, or my path clear cut, I might have written more and better poems, but my writing would have been less variegated (Greek: *poikílos*, whence the title, *Poikilopaidia*), and therefore less interesting. For the sake of that *poikilía*, I have included a small number of poems which might have fit more comfortably in a section devoted to juvenilia. But while my early poems were technically unpolished, they were not juvenile in thought. Besides, I did not begin to experiment with poetry before my sixteenth year, so, in a way, all my juvenilia were late—some, very late—perhaps even belonging to my second childhood.

One early exception was a four-line poem (lost) about a stag that loved a deer, which I handed, tongue-tied and trembling, to a blonde ten-year-old classmate. Another (melody included), composed by me at age three during a tedious car trip, went like this:

> *I'm a tired, a tired, a tired balloon.*
> *I went up too high, and came down too soon.*

That should be of interest to Jungian psychologists, as I had not yet read Greek mythology.

Even more remarkable, given such antecedent, is that I did not grow up to a life of Byronic dissipation. I owe that good fortune, aside from my lack of Byronic means, to the upbringing of my parents, and the example of my father, one of the rare and truly great poets of the virtuoso piano repertoire, and, like his equally great violinist brother, a wonderful human being. It is from them that I learned what art must do, and what so many have forgotten in spite of Rilke: *it must change you!*

I don't believe I came into my own voice until the mid-1970s, but looking back over the earliest poems, I can find hints of it there, too. The fact of the matter is that the poems I have collected in this volume represent a continuous and integral process, and one by which I seem to have acquired a most colorfully stippled education (*poikilopaidia*).

For that very reason, I have also opted against a separate section for translations. I have incorporated into the body of my original work a scattering of renditions from other-language poems *because they changed me*; and, as is only fair, *I changed them*. That is to say, I worked hard to make them English, accurate, and *mine*. Where I departed from their original sense or content, I have added a footnote, or inserted the word "after" before the name of the original author.

I did place one verse of my own invention (italicized in my translation—see page 49)—a wafer on the compliant tongue of the Roman philosopher-poet, Lucretius—to assert, humorously, if presumptuously, his approval of my handling of the jumbled introduction to his great poem on Epicurean physics. Indeed, I present herein for the first time to the lay public (it was previously published in *Rivista di Cultura Classica e Medioevale*, vol. 23 [1981], pp. 1-43, along with its supporting arguments), my translation of the Proem (verses 1 - 158) to *De Rerum Natura* (*On Nature*). The importance I give it is due to my having rearranged its seven constituent textual blocks into what I profess to be the correct order as left by the poet before the manuscript pages got scrambled in transmission. Various other scholars had tried their hand at rectifying the disorder in which those passages have come down to us, but none had managed, in spite of a great deal of eruditely specious argument, to reveal this notoriously daunting *Proemium* for the lucid rhetorical masterpiece that it is. There is only one way to reassemble an airplane. If it flies, it was put together right; if it doesn't, no amount of rationalizing will lift it into the air.

My poems are arranged in chronological order, with occasional concessions to topic, mood, or page layout. I was not consistent in dating my poems until around the year 2000, so in many cases I had to guess the year.

I have excluded from this collection my verse satire on Carl Sagan (*Professor Gansa's Dream*, 2003) and the several haiku contained in my as yet unpublished haiku novel, *Green Beetle Diaries*. These are self-standing works that should be judged on their own. The poem cycle, *At the Sign of the Swan*, included in this volume, will soon be available, God willing, as a separate booklet. The poems previously published in *Twilight with Halfmoon Rising*, including "Canto 7" from *Dante in Disneyland*, are included here with some revisions and corrections. As for the rest of *Dante in Disneyland*, until I have had a chance to recover and reassess something left tentative so long ago, I will only refer the reader to its opening lines:

> *In the middle of my life's great traffic jam*
> *I awoke to find myself on the wrong freeway.*

While some of my friends might take those verses as premonitory of my later return to Jewish observance and the mystical tradition of my ancestors, they would be jumping the gun. I see them rather as a contemporized theme song for the Wandering Jew.

P.G.

POIKILOPAIDIA

Patapon (1960).

Strange to begin with this poem, the only one I ever wrote in French. I wrote it for a girl I was in puppy love with for many years. I am a little ashamed of the poem, but Henry Miller, who made no secret of his dislike for poetry, found it charming, and often mentioned it. The way I came to write it is revealing. While in high school, I got a summer job as a sales clerk in a French bookstore in Westwood Village. On the display shelf was a children's book with a cartoon of a cuddly lamb on the cover. The title of the book was "Patapon", which seems to be a fairly common nom de tendresse. I lost my job at "Le Plaisir de France" when I gift-wrapped a customer purchase before checking the price sticker.

Patapon, Patapon,
où tu vas, nous y allons.
Soit en haut, soit en bas,
je te suis, je serai là.

Patapon, mon agnelette,
n'aie pas peur, ne t'inquiète!
Nous deux craignons ni vie ni mort.
Si tu t'appuis sur moi je serai fort.

Patapon, ma pauvre chérie,
Viens a moi, ton pauvre abri.
Je te rechaufferai quand tu as froid.
Colle-toi donc un peu contre moi!

Patapon, viens dans mes bras!
Souri et ri, et patatras . . . !
Plus de peines, plus de larmes . . .
Oui, les sourires et rires seront nos armes!

Patapon, ma belle et bête,
doute pas ton coeur, doute pas ta tête!
Je t'embrasserai, tu répondras . . .
Chut! et patati et patata . . .

Let Darkness Fall (1963)

Although I did not yet know how to write a sonnet, the sentiment is one that I can still identify with. Some 30 years later, at USC's Feuchtwanger Archives to look for my young correspondence with "Frau Marta", widow of the great novelist, I found a copy of this poem enclosed with a letter she had sent to poet-critic John Ciardi. I had read Ciardi's famous critical analysis of "Stopping by Woods on a Snowy Evening," and it was from Frost's lovely poem that I learned the technique, gamely attempted here, of repeating the final verse to strike overtones of deeper meaning.

Let darkness fall, then, on the land, that man
may homeward never see his way again,
nor mother, to the sobbing child. But this,
so all the nations of the earth might grope
themselves in darkness into one, and span
as with one pair of wings, one world of men.
Well might we sacrifice our eyes for this —
our useless, sightless eyes! — could we but hope
that palping, testing hands would never do
what our voracious eyes have led them to!
Let such a darkness come! and such a night
as could blot out what we have seen by light,
and we shall walk again with outstretched arms.
And we shall walk again with outstretched arms.

Still Reasoning with Me (July, 1969). Petrarca

Alone, distraught, the most forsaken field
I measure slowly, pace by halting pace,
my eyes downcast, prepared to turn my face
from where the sod with print of man is sealed.

Else, cover I find none, lest, face revealed,
I stand exposed before the populace.
For in my gestures, spent of all glad trace,
all may surmise how burns my blaze concealed.

So that I think the hills, the open vales,
the creeks and copses have by now descried
what friend and fellow still perceive too dim.

But where to seek such wild and surly trails,
I do not know, that love not keep my side
still reasoning with me, and I with him.

Orpheus (Feb. 11, 1971)

And sweetly pierced with life's unsparing sword
I wander, hands pressed tight against my wound
and leave my heart's blood dark upon the ground.
The poplar shades me, me the cypress grieves;
the willows bend to pluck my strings with leaves
and make away with one sweet stolen chord.
The earth thirsts after me, the air, my song;
my gravestone trails me like a famished wolf
and writes my epitaph upon itself.
The night laps up my dreams, the day my laughter;
birds harbinger my coming, worms writhe after.
Weeds ensnare my feet with clinging thong;
their rabid thorns tear souvenirs from my skin,
while all I love devours me from within.

Sea-Change (early 1970s)
The late poet Howard Nemerov rebuked me severely for daring to tread on William Blake's great poem with my unworthy feet.

Tiger, tiger,
prowling up the shore,
slinking easy, sly, grr —
growling with a roar . . .
Whiskers drool-drenched,
frothing at the maws,
rippling muscles cool-clenched,
lithe on liquid paws . . .
Hunching, haunching,
pouncing on your meat . . .
look — a kitten, purring
round and round my feet!

Musa Mea (1971 or '72)

My muse is small, and often she complains
when I would move the mountains with my words.
The shepherd's worth lies not in how his herds
have multiplied, but rather in what plains

he pastures them. The greatness of the Greeks
was that they spoke the people's common tongue,
and what they said was close to what they sung!
I wish I spoke the way my neighbor speaks . . .

Perhaps someday I'll have my little clan
of listeners who will value my two cents
and put up with the verbiage for the sense.

That would be quite enough. Who says a man
must speak his mind to multitudes out loud?
I say what's in me softly. Three's a crowd!

In Defense of Humanism (early 1970s)

All roads lead to Rome, or so we're taught;
so take the road your shoes are fitted for.
Some choose the steep crags of pragmatic thought,
but I prefer the peopled plains, the shore
where waves of history tumble and recede,
the mountain sediment that seaward flows.
Of higher vantage point I have no need
to scan the starry reaches of the sky
a mountain climber makes his living by.
My only map lies open at my toes.
All roads lead somewhere, though they seem to stray,
and few know when they've got there, anyway!
Besides, if Rome's the best of all abodes,
how come the Romans built so many roads?

Argos (1973)

In memory of Ralph Freed (1907-1973), one of the great popular songwriter-lyricists of the 1940s, and '50s.

Old friend, it seems like twenty years
since you've been gone
and I've been lying upon a bone . . .

Now and then I prick my ears
as if I hear you shuffling by . . .
and wag my tail and wake, and die.

Before a Japanese Print (1973 or '74)

The print was a Hiroshige woodblock I fell in love with in Perugia. I bought it on layaway.

An eagle sitting in a cherry tree
among the snow-white blossoms of new spring!
Winter's white claws have slipped where his now cling.
I gaze, daring to think that I am he!

Severely framed in a spare filigree
of branches, twigs and blooms – no other thing!
how patiently he waits with folded wing!
How still, how set apart, how starkly free!

Oh, I am not as handsome or as bold,
Nor do I cling with such tenacious claw.
Nor are my eyes as sharp or as far-seeing . . .

It is that I have known a spring as cold.
It is that no new spring can ever thaw
the blossom-tortured bleakness of my being!

Dolce Stil Novo (1972 or 73)

A sonnet that exploded like a star,
spewing out hot tongues of meaning all around;
songs like sweet Sumatran prunes from far,
that sucked for hours still burst with flavored sound;
a poem of alchemy, like cinnabar
that, warmed with human flames of understanding,
exudes elusive droplets of quicksilver
that in the fractal channels of the mind
forever keep contracting and expanding;
or like a woman's beauty unconfined
that zaps you with your first electric thrill of her —
I long for poetry of such a kind —
a bitter sweet and salty old-new style
that for one step will whirl you for a mile!

Thanksgiving (early 1970s)

*Se pareba boves, alba pratalia araba,
Alba versorio teneba, negro semen seminaba.*

— "*Indovinello Veronese*" (9th Century)

"He drove on his oxen, he plowed a white mead,
he held a white plow and he sowed a black seed."

And from those old furrows there sprang a rich crop,
a harvest undreamed of that grazed the rooftop.

For with that odd riddle a language was born
in which Alighieri might fittingly mourn.

But hear me interpret those riddle-me-rees:
My fingers were oxen, my meadows, the keys;

my piano, plow-heavy, my music, the seed —
black notes on the pages I hardly could read.

And yet, the sweet music grew on undeterred,
and now gushes forth in the form of the word.

Bucephalus (early 1970s)

This sonnet lay unfinished for many years. When the concluding couplet finally came to me, I burst out laughing.

After the first excruciating tries,
there came the time when, to his great surprise,
he proudly stood erect, noble, aloof,
exulting in the power of the hoof.
And then it was his shadow on the plain,
exquisite, vague, and dark, that gave him fear,
and threatened to unhorse the grand idea
astride him, ere it could give him the rein.
And so the poet with his godly gift
is apt from all his cherished dreams to drift
when, in the midst of something quite divine,
he stops and asks, "Where have I heard that line?"
Thus galloped off many a final couplet
into the credits and a flaming sunset!

To the Poet Who Said that Sappho Must Have had "Endemetriosis" (1973 or '74)

While studying the Greek lyric poets in Perugia, Italy, I borrowed from an American friend a volume of poems by Kenneth Rexroth. In it, I found a poem addressed to William Carlos Williams, in which Rexroth fatuously compares Williams to "the girls of the Anthology . . . not like strident Sappho / who for all her grandeur must have had endemetriosis." The stupid and offensive pun on Demeter riled me almost as much as the egregiously cavalier dismissal of one of the loveliest poets of antiquity. I thought of sending Rexroth my response, and might have done so had not my friend, confusing Rexroth with Frank O'Hara, told me that the former had died in an accident on Fire Island.

Could I concoct what malady I please
for *you*, I guess it would involve your prick,
changing what must be changed so far as sex.
But I should show more care than you in spelling

in order that the malady might stick.
And I should take my cue for such a hex
from symptoms manifest. I mean the swelling
of your head, filled with such idiocies.

Those who dare to pun the wings off bees
should not expect to come away unstung.
But crows must needs pick blind the nightingale.

Or did you think that thus you might inveigle
The muse to switch her lyre for yours unstrung?
Now go and diagnose your own disease!

To the Same, Calling Sappho "Strident"
(After an old fable told to me by my father.)

The nightingale, offended by the crow,
submitted to a challenge from her foe,

agreeing the first whom chance might send along
should be the judge and listen to their song.

The two of them in wrath decreed as prize
that he who won should pick the other's eyes.

Now chance would have it that the first to show,
of all things, was a pig, who could not know.

To such a one they gave the judge's cloak,
and he awarded victory to a croak.

And later, sobbing, shedding bloody tears,
the nightingale sits, when an owl appears,

who having heard the tale would feign console
the luckless bird with all that justice stole.

The songbird, whom Owl's gentle words exhaust,
prevents him, saying, "I cry not that I lost,

nor while I have an ear do I begrudge
the crow my eyes; *but that a pig should judge!*"

And here she gave a cry that pierced the heart
of all who hold some reverence for art.

An easy thing for you to ill-use her
whom twenty-five long centuries inter,

whose song has echoed down in tattered threads
that still entwine and tear my heart to shreds!

Were she alive, I think she would decline
to answer you. I'll make that honor mine,

and stake my living eyes for hers of dust,
and fill the holes with tears if so I must.

I'm not afraid. To me it's all one thing:
a crow may be my judge, if pigs may sing!

Better bards were blind than I pretend
to be, who lost their sight to lesser end.

Though mindful of my fable's truth, for her
I'd gladly run the risk that some will err

and honor flippant fools with such a prize,
if through my starless nights her songs could rise

in something of the splendor they hold hence.
But now that you have put in your two cents

and sung us what new songs make Sappho strident,
take these golden coins of hers—with my dent!

ODE TO APHRODITE (1971 or '72) Sappho
The meter is the Sapphic strophe.

Aphrodite, immortal on bright bedaubed throne,
playful child of god, I beseech you dearly:
Do not crush my soul with the pain of longing,
Lady, and sorrow.

Come to me, if ever on past occasion
you received my sighs from afar and answered,
stepping from the gold of your father's palace,
hastening hither.

Coupled you your carriage, and pretty sparrows
swiftly drew you over the earthly darkness,
whirring hard their wings from on high, amid the
heavenly aether.

And anon they came. And then you, O Blessed,
radiant with a smile on your face immortal,
you would ask me, What is the matter now, then?
Why do I call you?

What with all my might do I wish for now, then,
in my madness? "Whom shall I now win over
sweetly to thy tender endearment, who now,
Sappho, rejects thee?

"Does she shun thee? Lo, she shall soon pursue thee!
Gifts she will have none? Yet she gifts shall offer!
Loves she not? Yet even anon she shall love!
Yea, notwithstanding!"

Come to me now, too, in distress and free me
from my plight! Whatever my heart desires,
make my wish come true! And for just this once more,
be my accomplice!

Asylum (1972 or '73)

Personal opinion, private taste
make sacred fortresses of ready use,
where all retire, laying the nation waste
when knowledge puts the ignorant to rout.
In ancient times, so served the house of Zeus,
where miscreants seeking a strong redoubt
might make a dash—not for cathartic rapture,
but for the expedient of avoiding capture.
And most religions since the pagan days
afforded some degree of such immunity
for those who sought not truth, but just impunity.
Taste is a temple ignorant folk raise.
But the entrance to their shrine is strait, alas,
and ignorance too gross to ever pass!

On Reading Eliot's Introduction to Pound (early 1970s.)

Dear Eliot, you should be penny-wise
    if you're so damned Pound-foolish!
Your prose leaves you as naked, anywise,
    as Pound's verse leaves me coolish.

Your robes to Pound like a penny found,
    O Thomas Stearns, goddemmit,
you'd think a stooge could be more scrooge —
    even an anti-Semite!

Film Criticism (early 1970s)

When you claim your slice of free speech,
    you open your mouth wide,
but plug it with your camera,
    and speak from your backside.
I love free speech, but wonder how
    they ever let you pass —
with camera stuck in your mouth,
    projector up your ***.
The actors, too, went much too far,
    hoping to make a hit.
How sad to want to be a *
    and then to end up **** !

Snails and Ships (early 1970s)

Like twin Cupids playing with bow and arrow,
each shoots his dart into the other's marrow.
the deadly arms they make their playthings of
take their effect and turn their war to love!

Old ships at war might thus seem to make love —
a pirateer to which her captive's hove.
So, sometimes lovers bound by an affair o'
the heart discover love has turned to war, oh!

Indovinello (early 1970s)

Thou Genii of the Lamp, thou Bird-in-Cage
who flutterest round inside in a white rage,
thou Mother's Son of Man, compressed, constrained
in the small universe thou hast obtained,
I know that thou wouldst serve and soar and make
of thyself a sacrifice for my sake,
but we are in analogous designs
and each must suffer in his own confines.

Life's Art (The first line is from 1975; the rest from 2019)

Life's art of taking aught from naught
   would seem to leave us with a minus —
ironically, since the process ought
    to shape and polish and refine us!

Water Music (early 1970s)

I go and seek the level water seeks —
my own. No matter if I often stumble.
Water falls and learns thus to be humble
and to make music every time it speaks.

Far Lights (1973 or '74) For Mario Martini

The sentry solo of a neon light
draws my restless life down to the hills
toward the valley, down to Ponte Rio
at the bluest moment of the night,
when Jupiter, hung molten, slowly chills
and all becomes transparent and unreal.
I'm walking home by Via Sperandio.
The chorus of my path is still. The air
is cool and soft like a split cantaloupe.
Far lights. Strangers at their evening meal.
I press my soul against each yellow square
like banished fire lured home by moths of hope
and think of all the places I have been.
I guess my lot is outside looking in.

Dialogue Before a Tomb at Cesri* (May 28-29, 1970)
For Mario Martini

Spider, that defend with web the thoughtful tomb
where proud Etruscans leaned on cubital of stone,
what despatches have you from the fragrant broom
that you should thus adorn these cool and noble portals?
Can your office be to guard these peaceful harbors
even though the ships once moored therein are gone?
No treasure is secure behind your silken thread!
Perhaps you think the importunate will fear your bite
or that it's you who keep at bay the piercing light?
Or would you serve reminder to forgetful mortals
that, tenuous as are the bonds that hold the dead,
equally so are those that bind to life the living?

Philosopher, that wander through these lofty arbors,
no prize has ever issued from behind my weaving,
though many are the riches that have passed within.
I spread my net across a stream that ever flows —
of life, of hope, of dream, of spirit and desire
and catch the tiny dewdrops fallen from that breath.
For only truth will cling unto the web I spin —
and beauty. These I string as beads on silver wire.
When one is filled, I weave another of my rows.
And even as your thoughts were plundering this tomb,
I gleaned from them whatever I could save from death
and wove therefrom an ageless pattern on my loom.

*Cesri was the Etruscan name for Cerveteri.

Meeting (1973 or '74)
for Marcella Massidda and Pippíu

Horse, have you an ear for human woe?
Or are you merely eyes with question round
and hooves that lightly tread upon the ground
with prehistoric toe?

Oh yes, we have the gentle touch, we do!
Our eyes, our limbs, betray a kind of soul
that were not foreign to a purebred foal
or to a wandering Jew.

Brothers (though of different stripe and state)
by virtue of the partnership we lack —
for Jews are not accustomed to your back
nor you to Jewish weight —

you listen to my words without replying
the way I watch you gallop o'er the sod:
you think you are conversing with a god,
and I, that I am flying.

Speculation (early 1970s)

I had read a review — most likely in Time Magazine *— of a book whose thesis, according to the reviewer, was that the history of the Middle Ages was determined by the horse. I had just devoted several years to acquiring the somewhat less simplistic notion that history is determined by humans. As fond as I am of horses, and as ready to acknowledge their historical role, I was peeved to think that a member of* Homo sapiens sapiens *should write a book propounding a hippocentric view of history. Americans have little patience for history and are generally content to find a simple formula by which to encapsulate it. The following sonnet encapsulates my reaction.*

If Eohippus had not grown so tall,
and if his evolutionary curve
did not through Providence so coincide
with Man's, then many had been spared a fall;
for if the rider lost his grip or nerve,
he'd simply jack his feet down either side.
History would have ploughed a different course —
or hoed — and been a humbler, happier farmer.
Not so much fear would Macedonian horse
have struck in Athens' hearts; and knights in armor
could not have gone so far in clanking rivalry,
or brought in the Dark Ages with their chivalry!
But, little fellow, you were not too small
for Man if he can blame a horse for all . . . !

A New Noah (February or March, 1974)

In February, 1974, the world was stunned to learn that the great Russian writer, Alexander Solzhenitsyn, had been arrested by the Soviet Government. I wrote two poems while we waited with bated breath to hear what would become of him. Thanks to the universal outcry, the Soviet authorities opted to send him into exile, rather than into the cellar.

You wrote the word in blood upon the walls
that cut off man from man, and then you said
the word will go the day the stonework falls,
and with that fall raise up again the dead.
But one drop of this man's courageous blood
will wash from those heraldic walls the word
and weigh upon the graves of the interred
with stones that human hands shall never lift,
like stone that once beat in a human breast
and lies submerged beneath the red wave's crest.
A new Noah floats upon that crimson flood!
Now is the raven forth and Man adrift!
Go, olive leaf, and show him land is nigh,
or haven for the dove, if he should die!

Archipelago

Go back a longer lapse of years,
    or else more dead people ago
and Gulag no longer appears
    a lonely archipelago,
but just one of a Cyclades
    (perhaps one of the main)
of demons, devils, spies, De Sades,
    of darkness, lies, and pain.
For your Gulag and my Hades
    will surely someday gel
and form from all the suffering
    one integrated hell.
But men like you appear to dwell
    upon a magic island
(perhaps one of the Sporades?)
    where, for a hopeful spell,
  our hearts are our authorities,
    called Speak-Truth-and-Defy-Land!

S'I' Fosse Foco (1975?) Cecco Angiolieri (ca 1260 – 1312)

If I were flame, I'd set the world on fire;
if I were wind, I'd tempest-blow it down;
if I were water, I would let it drown;
if I were God, I'd damn it to hellfire.

If I were Pope, then what a jolly friar!
for I'd turn all of Christendom upside-down.
If I were king, how would I wear my crown?
I'd chop your heads clear off, did you enquire.

If I were death, I'd visit my old man;
if I were life, why then, from him I'd flee;
and I'd do likewise for the old woman.

If I were Cecco, as I am and be,
I'd take as many pretty girls I can,
and leave the ugly ones to charity!

Fool's Prayer (mid-1970s)

Oh God! With troubled mind and sinful flesh,
I still, with all my lacerated heart,
desire, as long I'm clothed in human guise,
to speak my lines and so fulfil my part.
Forgive, if much takes place behind the wings
between the times the fool who plays the wise
trips out onstage, gesticulates and sings,
that was not ever meant for eyes to see,
and makes a soul unworthy of its task.
The mule of man's revolving days must thresh
the wheat of life unto the fall of dusk:
in course, the kernel's trodden with the husk.
I pray that if pretense must fall from me,
my face might prove no meaner than my mask.

To Myself (1975?)

(After a sonnet by Guido Cavalcanti, thought to have been addressed to Dante Alighieri.)

I come to thee each day infinite times,
and find thy thoughts immersed in turpitude;
and I am filled with sorrow for thy noble mind
and many virtues that so leave thee nude.

Thou used to shun the vulgar of mankind,
disdained to curry favor with the crude.
Thou held me in thy heart so well defined,
I gathered in thy steps the poems thou strewed.

Now for the lewdness of thy life, I dare
no more profess to like thy way of speech,
or suffer thee to soil me with thy gaze.

Yet will I always stay within thy reach . . .
If thou couldst only see how close we are,
and how perversely thou dost turn away!

Letter to Miss Lonely Hearts (1973?)

A found poem: I translated it from an advice column in an Italian women's magazine I was looking at while getting a haircut.

I am twenty-three.
Two years ago
I went for six months
with a young man
I loved very much
who left me
telling me cruelly
he was seeing someone else.
You too will understand
that I can't let go,
that I have tried everything to see him again.
And finally, he did agree
to give me an explanation.

He told me he left me
because I want us to get married
but he doesn't want to be hitched.
Sometimes I see him from my window
because he drives his car
past where I work.
Do you think he still loves me?
I shall never be able to forget him,
or think of another man.

To a Blonde (1973 or '74)

Not long after writing the following, I wrote a palinode, using the same rhyme scheme and rhymes. It was clever, but rather nasty, so I destroyed it.

You flaming Blonde! You star! I'd love to know . . .
how many times has Homo sapiens
unleashed on you the solar metaphor?
But none, I'll bet, has ever used a lens
to focus it upon your heart before,
in hidden hope of setting it ablaze!
For while it's you we credit with the rays,
it's we, in fact, who're smoldering below!

So really you're more like the focal point
of all the rays of what own light I've got.
But I shall blow these ardent words your way
to fan to flame that tiny blazing spot!
O flaming sun, you bring the light of day
to many gloomy lives, and as you rise,
you always delicately paint the skies
of all whose brow your golden rays anoint.

And when you sink beyond the happy arc
whose noon you've been, you set, not as you dawned,
but in a blaze of jealousy and lust!
So I don't wish that we were one, dear blonde,
but that, united through my mortal dust
with all your earthly lovers, I could form
a globe — revolving, always keeping warm
the sunny side and cooling off the dark!

The Wind and the Soap Bubble (1973 or '74)

The metre is the Latin elegiac couplet, consisting of the dactylic hexameter followed by the pentameter. I added a Romantic touch by rhyming the two hemistichs of the pentameter.

Once, as I lay in the shade of a leaning oak, reading Leibniz,
    glancing aloft in surprise, I beheld a delight to the eyes:
floating languidly by flew a soap bubble blown by an infant
    playing somewhere not far away—games that I, too, used to play.
Perfect, round, and suffused with the liquid colors of Iris,
    lightly sustained by the air, just out of reach, "If you dare,
catch me, or try!" said the sphere, but before I could rise, lo, the wind did;
    and, while I sat there entranced, the wind and the soap bubble danced!
Oh, how they danced, how they whirled, how they bobbed and dipped
    through the aether!
    Each was something sublime, waltzing through space and through time.
Iced-over dreams melted into the brim-full cup of my sorrows,
    till, with the warmth of the wind, the wine in my goblet had thinned.
Then came a doleful sigh through the leaves in the branches above me.
    Downward filtered a voice. To listen was hardly a choice!
"Ah, woe is me, who have had my will of the world through the ages!
    I, in whose way nothing stood, whether for evil or good,
I, who hold sway over land and sea, over all of Creation,
    ushering in rain or sun, flushing out clouds for the fun,
I, who, if so I had wished, could have swept you away with a brief puff,
    whisking you off to my lair by your oak-green-ribboned hair,
I, who am uncontested laird of the globe, am defied by . . .
    Yes! By a bubble of soap—tinted with heliotrope!
So said the wind to the oak with a sob and a choke, and was silent.
    But I and the leaves up above knew that the wind was in love.
And, I was touched by the plight of the wind, for 'twas all too familiar:
    No matter which way he blew, whether askant or atrue,

nor how fierce nor how soft, such froth would always elude him,
> turning his every advance into a twist of her dance.

Meanwhile, a lull had descended, drowsy with warmth and with fragrance,
> casting a spell on the deep bosom of nature asleep.

Still stood the tree for a pregnant pause, while I waited and wondered.
> Then, with a wind-borrowed sigh, rustled the leafy reply:

"O my impetuous friend, I knew this was bound to befall you!
> Love spares no one the pain of loving someone in vain.

Some things life has in store that can't be possessed without losing.
> This you, too, had to learn; now it is simply your turn.

Oh, do not howl in despair! In a sense, you shall keep her for always —
> if so long can endure something so frail and so pure.

For in the dance that you wove she was yours more than you can imagine!
> That is the charm of romance: *true* love is only a dance!"

What did the wind respond with a whisper of leaves in the treetops?
> I didn't hear what he said, but saw the oak bow her head.

For, with an aching heart he rose up to pursue his beloved,
> combing the glen and the grass for a bright gleam as of glass.

Dance while the music plays, O lovers, dance to the music!
> Soon the musicians will tire, soon will pack up and retire.

Then, like the wind, you will search without end, for alas he had lost her—
> even the while the wind died, stalled by the blow to his pride.

Yes, while he whinged and whined to the wise, old oak of his misery,
> the bubble began to descend, long overdue for an end.

"*Where is she?*" shrieked the enraged wind into the shivering branches.
> I could have told, but I durst not, for the bubble had burst.

Choreography for a Dream (1974 or '75)

I dreamed I was a blasted heath
and she came dancing like the lightning,
laughing o'er the ruin beneath;
and when my ashes soiled her shoes,
she loosed their ethery sinews;
and then I felt her laces tight'ning
round my neck, and thought I'd choke
with ecstasy—until they broke . . .

I dreamed I was a moonlit mire
and she played like a will-o-wisp
upon my body with cold fire;
and when the gauze she wore had burned,
she leapt up naked, flashed and turned
and vanished with an airy lisp;
and then I burned with icy fever
and wept it did not last forever . . .

I dreamed I was a rocking ocean,
she, a breeze lying on my breast,
and both locked in ecstatic motion;
and when the billows reached the shore,
our breath and brine mixed with a roar
and foamed into a frothy crest
and crashed together on the beach
and boiled as far as I could reach . . .

I dreamed I was a gliding stream:
A cloud peered into my smooth mirror
and seemed to swim as in a dream.
the mirrored cloud in me was love,
though she flew undisturbed above.
I did not think I was in error,
but lovingly I bathed the lie
in my own lymph as it slid by . . .

I dreamed I was these things and more,
and she answered my every change
with something finer than before —
until I dreamed she was my dream,
dancing variations on a theme
that spanned a never-ending range;
and while she danced, I made a leap
and caught her close, and fell asleep . . .

NON EXPLICIT PAUSA EST

Poikilopaidia (1973)

I must have written this when I first conceived the idea of publishing all of my poems in a single collection, rather than piecemeal.

What the title means, you ask. Let's see . . .
Several meanings vie to volunteer,
and you may pick the one you think I'd use.
Now, as for *poikilos*, there we agree:
veined and marbled, like a column tier,
or richly colored with a range of hues.
The rest is more a question of the accent:
Paidía denotes knowledge, letters, learning;
hence, my encyclopedia, for a start,
a book of flowers, rainbowed, if they lack scent,
or else my own mythology of yearning,
embracing the instruction of my heart.
But in the event you're not hiring a tutor,
remember that *paidía* could be neuter.

Neuter plural, the homophone means children,
which lends a new shape to the title's cloud,
and makes me neither Bullfinch nor song-filled wren,
but a doting father, anxious, proud,
perhaps unduly hopeful for his brood.
What's that? You say you have no room for kids —
even as few and well-behaved as mine?
(Long have I toiled to keep them well in line!)
Then let the accent move as humble bids,
so that another sense is now accrued:
for *paidiá* means child's play, trifles, ploys.
Amuse yourself with my discarded toys.
And yet, be careful they do not inspire
too much confidence: I play with fire.

Dedication (1973)

Well might scholars rake my scattered leaves
where winds of autumn shall have blown in vain,
and gather them in neat and careful sheaves
according to their color and their vein.

Or else remove them from the hallowed ark
of centuries and let them decompose!
But while those leaves still cling to living bark,
I ask no more than any tree that grows.

And granted that, what Providence achieves
is no concern of mine in sun and rain,
so long as I may shelter some sweet lark
of poetry and feed some grub of prose.

I am, with all my xylem and my phloem,
a poet: I can spare the worms a poem!

Table of Contents (1973)

To those who picnic now beneath my shade,
I say *bon appétit* with a fresh breeze.
It makes no difference how the cloth is laid,
for here, you'll find all sorts of delicacies.

The present tense devours all things piecemeal,
and barely takes the time to lick its thumbs.
So nibble on what offers most appeal:
there's everything from odes to conundrums.

Before the memory of this hour can fade,
time's legions will emerge in slim sorties
and make a nine-course banquet of your meal.
So is one man's feast another's crumbs!

But scholars, too, survive by that same lesson:
tomorrow dines where we delicatessen . . .

Manifesto (mid-1970s; revised)

Roar low into the ground and let the vibes
carry forewarning, backed by bite and claw,
to all the near and distant forest tribes
that there's still something in the jungle's law

approaching justice, if, with lion's heart
the poet, to whom mere speech is life, and truth
an afterlife, and art — well, what is art
if not his mask of God? — will swear an oath

that all this hogwash that the world imbibes
shall neither spoil his aim nor stay his paw
from striking square at all that sets apart
man from man; and clear the undergrowth

at last of small fry, so the jungle floor
may vibrate to the wounded lion's roar!

The Lion's Share (mid-1970s); previously published in *Twilight with Halfmoon Rising*.

The lion's share is not without its wound —
the existential gash that is the gaping
knowledge that there can be no escaping
the most original of sins compounding
man: to have extracted from surrounding
nothingness some joy! But being so carved
in cochleid bas relief, not in the round,
I want that column to be mine — the wharved
pure thrusting naked symbol of man's raping
dreams inside the ravished universe —
not for myself, like some forever aping
future monuments with fictive fronds,
but to evoke with all-embracing verse
hot waves of truth until the void responds . . .

To a Portrait of Sheryl (mid-1970s)

Ockham's razor, Alexander's sword
were each too dull to cleave "I know" from "I";
and even Love, before he drew his cord
would hardly know what tip he should apply.

I know your beauty is no more your own
than of this photograph, though it demurs:
"The splendor that you see, I hold on loan;
by grace it shines from me, but it is hers."

And I reply, as Alexander might,
"Give me those words from her own lips on mine,
and Eros' bow may spare me Aphrodite!"
Yet I can't name what cleaving can't define!

A sword of Damocles revolves above;
but only breathe, it falls and sighs, "I love!"

Paolo's Reproach (1976 or '77)
Translated from verses by Paolo Montalbini, Professor of Patologia Vegetale at the Università degli Studi di Perugia, addressed to me in Italian. The original is lost.

I write you these few lines:
but think of them as if I had not written.
Consider them, that is, as if they were not;
and when you read them,
pretend you have not read them.
If you would write me a few lines,
consider it done.
I shall think of them
as if you had not written.
That is, as if they were not.

Song Without Words (1976 or '77)
to Paolo Montalbini

Because the words were always few
and far between
the two of us and immaterial
I remember the ductile silences
that swathed us like a pair of cats
embalmed in karmic pyramids
visualize the ivory outlined anapests
of gauntly solipsistic walks
in *Corso delle Vergini Stralunate*
the faceless push and clatter of the student mess
unearthed in the phantasmagoric factory
where they once manufactured suitcases
whose voyages have long since ceased
under the ancient shadows of the aqueduct.
    I grew accustomed to your speechlessness
could sum the desultory spans of your hanging sentences
with a gesture of fatality
or a beat of comedic syncopation.
    But there were also mantled silences
that could have bent to breaking the boughs of words
that time would melt to water too high for speech.
The rising falls submerged our *tête-à-têtes*
in ecstasies of stereo string quartets
prolonged our solemn *spaghettate alle vongole*
with cold *Verdicchio* from your tacit soil
our ears made drunk with the melancholy strains
of suave Vivaldi verecund and vibrant
and the tall windows yielded thankfully
to the evening breeze wafting soft through the sleeping fields
ushering in the glimmer of far Assisi
like a waiting bride on the slope of dark Subasio.
    Granted: hidden beneath your taciturnity
the retort of your much dissembled wit –
Brutus made bold by a convivial *bicchierin*,
the unsuspecting felled after a pause

by the afterbite of meek decoctions
bitter as sin, revenge of austere monks.
    Or amongst your tomes on the pustulent rots
the pestilential cankers
that scourge the turbid and tumultuous world of plants
a demure passion for philosophy and art.
    But Paolo, still the talk was of dubious consequence,
a mute companionship of scavengers
of benighted bachelors.
The passing years composed an odd dialogue
your travail conversing unheard with mine
so that it seemed almost a sacrilege
to plot with the calipers of our defeat
the course that we have always known was etched in stone.
    And yet, if upon some astral or glacial plane
we abjured the storied rubbleheaps, the babbled ruins,
we did not serenely gull the prelingual blue skin
of oceans yearning beyond fathom
but as the afflicted souls of penitents
might yearn to assume the flesh of creeping things,
so our chastened words
like uncomplicated creatures
ungoverned by much reason, unacquainted
with pressing purpose,
did their intermittent and antic dance
arcanely choreographed by the intelligence
that planned our infinitely diverging parallels.
    Yes. Well to consider this as though not written
as though not read or if read as though forgotten.
But if some day (as I used to importune him)
the most utterable of saints, friend of fools
counsellor of wolves and of the wordless
should blow through the windows of your grief a woman
lovely as friendship, patient as conversation
and as women will she besiege your quiet mien
with fragile engines of elaborate reproach,
bring these lines forth resonant from somewhere
transparent with all that a friend can say without words

before you commence to disremember
this letter which is not, is not,
these vagrant words which from time to time
and so forlornly
raise their hand in semblance of a greeting.

Fog (date unknown) Hermann Hesse

Strange to wander in the fog!
Apart is every bush and stone.
No tree can see the other.
Each one is alone.

For me the world was full of friends,
when in my life the light shone.
But now that the fog descends,
I am friend to no one.

Truly, no man is wise
who does not know the dark.
The inescapable, the soul of things
looks him in the eyes.

Strange, to wander in the fog . . .
to live is to be lonely.
No man knows another.
Each is one – one only.

Aias (early 1980s?) Vincenzo Cardarelli. (1887 - 1959). Previously published in *Twilight with Halfmoon Rising*.

Oblivious always, Telamonian Aias,
of prudence in war and prayer,
thou never thought to invoke the aid
of a kindly goddess
who should almightify thy strength
or solicitous from the foe subtract thee.

Thou hadst no mother
to soften Olympus to thy destiny,
discreetest hero,
nor to thee was it given
to accomplish deeds of wanton grandeur,
to trip up Mars or Hector,
or wound the pinkie of Aphrodite.
But combat, barbarous and horrid,
against crushing odds and opponents,
in days that love not to be remembered.
When Zeus was bilious
with the Achaians,
to thee to go down to battle,
worthy spawn of Sisyphus,
seedling of Titans.
When raging Mars
led the Trojan ranks
against the ships with fire,
thou rescued them and Teucer.
Thou wast the great reserves
in the extremest peril,
the resistance, the wall, the fortress.
Every evening bade thee welcome
thy naked tent
without perfumes or panting slaves.
There, in a paste of dust and blood,
thou slept thy animal, hard sleep.
First among thine own,
of what many heroes convened before Ilion
second to none.
But verily alone
and unique wast thou
in adversity.
By no god protected,
by no unwrestled glory smiled upon,
thy valor alone thine escort,
fighter of yore.
And the Greeks denied thee
the prize thou coveted:
Achilles' arms. A master of intrigues
snatched them away. But to the sea
he lost them. And the pious wave,

the fickle wave, more wise
than human judgement, constant more
than fortune,
upon they heap of earth at last reposed
them. Peace to thy soul,
indomitable Aias! *

> *The original has *Pace all'anima tua / infera, Aiace*: literally, "Peace to thy soul / underworld, Aias. But *infera* also suggests the Latin *ferus*: wild, untamed.

Hymn to Venus and Proem to the *De Rerum Natura* of Lucretius
(1974 or '75) *Turbae sodali Perusinae sacrum.*

The manuscript tradition of these introductory verses (1-158) has left us with an obviously jumbled version of what was, in its pristine condition, a great rhetorical masterpiece. Many scholars have gone way out on one limb or another to defend the incoherent order of passages in which the proem has come down to us. Others, supposedly including Cicero, have searched unsuccessfully for the correct order of the seven main blocks of text passages that stand out for their internal coherence. My rearrangement and translation of those passages follows below. The argument in support of this reconstruction is set forth at length in my article, "De rerum natura proemium restitutum," *in* Rivista di Cultura Classica e Medievale, *vol. 23 (1981), pp. 1-43. I am forever grateful to the late Ettore Paratore, Director of the* Rivista, *and to the late Umberto Pizzani, Professor of Latin Literature at the* Università degli Studi di Perugia *and my cross-examiner at the disputation of my Tesi di Laurea, for championing this work in spite of the indignation of various academics (particularly the late Francesco Giancotti of the* Università di Bologna) *who never forgave me for making this discovery while still a student.*

[vv. 1 - 43]
Foremother of our Roman seed,
delight of gods and men,
Venus, on whom all life doth feed,
who beneath the lapse of heav'n
peoplest the seas with ships and rowing,
the fields of earth with fruitful sowing,
to thee all living things, indeed,
once risen and conceived, are owing
that see the light of day.

Thee, Goddess, flee the winds, and thy
coming the heaven's cloud;
to thee offers sweet flowers, shy,
the busy earth unplowed;
for thee shines the sea's smiling level
and serene the skies in soft light revel;
no sooner can day Spring descry
or vital breezes, loosed, bedevil,
gently holding sway,

than thee, Divine, thine entering,
touched to the very heart,
first signify the beasts of wing
all-vibrant with thy art.
Then skip wild herds o'er happy mead,
braving the river's swollen speed.
Thus prey to lust, each living thing
must thee pursue where thou wilt lead,
and howsoe'er it may

And then o'er sea and mountain and
across rapacious flood,
in each birdsnest through leafy wood,
o'er greening meadowland,
inflicting love on every breast,
sweet love on all, thou effectest
that kind by kind and brood by brood
they propagate their clay.

Because thou governest alone
the nature of the world,
nor without thee may blade nor stone
come forth or be unfurled,
nor anything be made content,
nor aught be pleasing, thou absent,
join in the verses I intone!
Be thou allied in my intent
on nature to essay —

for Memmius, our loving friend,
whom thou hast willed undaunted
to excel wherever he contend,
vict'ry-adorned, and vaunted.
So much the more, bestow, Divine,
eternal charm on every line;
and meanwhile have thou quietened
the savage works of wartime, daunted
sea and land away.

For thou alone canst benefit
with tranquil peace poor mortals,
since he, in mighty armor fit,
who openeth the portals
of savage war is wont to lie,
Mars, in thy bosom languidly,
o'erwhelmed with love's eternal wound.
So, craning his smooth neck around
to see thy face above,
He feasts his eyes on thee with love,
and gapes in sheer dismay.

Ah yes! His very breath, it seems,
depends from thy bent brow.
Envelope him, thy holy limbs,
recumbent on thee now;
pour little words sweet from thy mouth,
woo peace, alone which Rome endow'th;
else, in these times iniquitous
our promised task doth envy us
the peace of mind we pray.

Nor, Scion of famed Memmius' blood,
such things being so inclined,
may we neglect the public good
where it lieth enshrined.

[vv. 80 - 101] And in these straits, 'tis this I fear,
lest thou should to thyself appear
bound on a path of traitorhood,
where impious elements might rear
their head and thee waylay.

The contrary! On just such deeds
and other impious acts,
religio more often feeds,
shall we consider facts:
In Aulis, Iphigenia
upon the thrice-named virgin's
altarstone, the lords of Greece,
in whom the flower burgeons
of men, of heroes, lo! the chosen,
to sacrilegious slaughter cozen.
Her maiden brow the holy band
encircles, trails a double strand
upon her cheeks, astray.

And when she sees that by the shrine
her grieving sire doth stand,
and close by him his ministers
in vain conceal the brand,
and at her sight the people weep,
then, meek and mute, she sinks knee-deep,
seeking the earth, trembling, forlorn,
in vain her father-king's first-born;
for men's hands lift her in a heap
and bear her to the dais.

So comes she to the altarplace:
not, done the sacred, solemn
rites as wont, to take her place
in hymenaeal column;
but chaste, unchastely in cold slaughter,
victim, to die her butcher's daughter,
that fortunate and with good grace
a fleet might sail upon the water,
on her marriage-day!

[vv. 62 - 79]
>Of so much crime Religion could
humanity persuade!
But when the human brotherhood
lay vilely oppressed and weighed
to earth by her before all eyes,
and from the region of the skies
she hung, showing men her ugly head,
a Greek first dared to raise his eyes,
first could she not affray!

>Him neither hearsay of a god,
him neither thunderbolt
nor murmur'd menace overawed
from heaven's rumbling vault
but, nay! that spurred him on the more
to challenge nature's narrow door.
So ardent as to break the bolt,
his will prevailed, first to explore
the world that yonder lay!

>He skirted far its flaming wall
and with his soul and mind
roamed far o'er the unmeasured all,
whence, victor to mankind,
what may be born he doth relate,
and what may not, and in what state
each finite power of every kind
by high decree must terminate
and each come into play.
Wherefore Religion underfoot
is crushed into the clods,
and vict'ry doth now us promote
equals beside the gods!

[vv. 44-49]
>(The nature of these beings doth spell
that they, far from our cares,
enjoy the height of peace and dwell
cut off immortal eras;
for free from pain and peril made,
each on his own resources fares,
nor need they us, nor are they swayed
by our deserts, nor at our errors
touched by wrath are they).

[vv. 102–126] But thou, no matter what the times,
wilt seek to turn from us,
soon overwon by fearsome rhymes
of seers unscrupulous.
How many stories they can weave
to ruin thy life beyond retrieve,
thy fortune spoilt, thou timorous!
Nor wonder! Could men but believe
an end to affliction's day,

then some reason had made thee strong
to stand up to the seers
with all their woe-betiding song
and flummery in thy ears.
But now men lack means to rebel,
fearing eternal pain in hell,
ignoring, other things among,
what be the nature of the soul,
if it be born or nay,

or if it enter us at birth
and die with us together,
to haunt the darkness in the earth
in hell's lagoons, or whether
to join another living being,
as our own Ennius doth sing,
who first from Helicon's sweet berth
the crown of glorious frond did bring
on Roman brow to lay.

Yea, Ennius, who in deathless verse
expounds on Acheron,
whose shores nor soul nor body nurse,
he nonetheless says on,
but some weird kind of pallid wraith,
whence Homer, thriving still, he saith,
arose, revealed the world in verse,
and all the while salt tears did bathe
the form he did display!

[vv. 50-61]   Thou see'st how nothing doth remain
                 but, purged thine ear of lies, for
              thee to apply thy nimble brain
                 to Reason's enterprise.
              Nor spurn my gifts ere comprehended,
                 ranged as I in faith intended;
              for I commence the ways of heav'n
                 and gods, all hesitation ended.
                    To thee I shall portray

              primordial dust, whence nature all
                 createth, groweth, feedeth,
              and whither those same things dissolved,
                 conversely, nature leadeth:
              called "matter", "generative germs", (these
              being for reason's use rough terms) and
              "seeds of things", too, we them call, and
                 "primal corpuscles", for all
              things thence derive their trait.

[vv. 127-158]   And therefore, 'twill be well, as soon
                   we've touched on things supernal,
                the paths of sun and moon,
                   nocturnal and diurnal,
                and what goes on, and by what reason,
                here on earth, then 'twill be season
                about the mind and soul to learn all:
                   of what consisting, whence arisen,
                      wisely to assay.

              And what things come upon our mind
                 in terror and in torment,
              when wakeful, when to bed confined,
                 and what when we lie dormant —
              so that we seem to see and hear
                 as if in person, and as near,
              those who we know are dead and gone,
              of whom earth hugs the banished bone
                 where they lie tucked away.

Nor does it take me unawares
that it is hard to render
Latin verse these Grecian wares
obscure: many engender
need of words, the poverty
of tongue to blame, the novelty
of topic. But thy bravery eggs
me on, thy cherished friendship begs
me to no more delay:

Whatever be the task at hand,
in placid, night-time vigil,
to seek what words and how best scanned
and what poetic sigil
I should adopt to shed clear light
upon thy mind, that fully might
thou all that's hid survey.

Because this terror and this darkness
within the mind 'tis meet
should be dispelled not by the starkness
of brilliant day's sun-beat,
but by the face and rationale
of nature, whose first principle
shall hereunto be thus set out:
that nought may ever come of nought,
not e'en the gods to obey.

For mortals thus fear overawes
and holds in terror's clasp:
they see so much on earth whose cause
by no means can they grasp;
and so they think 'tis some god's will.
Wherefore, when we have seen that nil
may come of nil, what we pursue
we shall behold in surer view:
a world not made by gods!

Comic Strip, Fikellura Style (1975?)

"Semper me fugio et insequor,"
would seem to say the naked pygmy, running
round his amphora with a smile of cunning
at being behind himself and yet before.

And ever will he flee and yet give chase,
for should he tire of being himself's own victim,
so pleased it his creator to depict him,
he need not execute an about-face

for suddenly the hunted to play hunter.
Or, if he weary of being persecutor,
his quarry will oblige, and be his suitor.
So fine the craftsman's point! Need I be blunter?

Thus have I always lived! Such is my temper!
Insequor et fugio me semper!

Golgotha (1973 or '74)

You see, dear, love and beauty do not mix.
A woman's beauty is her crucifix.
The tenderest look of a desiring male
is like the jab of yet another nail.
His softest flattery is like a spear
that prods her in the ribs, although sincere.
While he who loves performs his Stabat Mater,
she whom he loves drinks vinegar for water.
But I am nailed upon a cross of love:
Your beauty is what my nails are fashioned of!
So that each has the other crucified
at his own sorely mutilated side.
Neither a Christ, but rather flanking thieves;
neither the other, each but himself deceives.

Appendix (mid-1970s)

The toxins tippled with such grim sobriety
in the crass, concentric coils of our society
collect in the most vulnerable appendage
to the entrails of this lets-pretend age
where they erupt, contaging the sublime
with uncommitted or committed crime.
Shall not such adjuncts to collective life
deliberately be cut out by the knife,
torn from the bowels like something morganatic,
disposed of in a kind of organ attic
where feelings, floating in their own denial
find parodies of peace, each in its phial?
Behold the man, albeit cut and dried,
seen through a bottle of formaldehyde!

Algernon (1973 or '74)

This happened in Terracina, Italy, where I had gone to my Uncle Bronislaw's beach house to recover from a nasty confrontation over my Dissertation and to study for an upcoming exam. There were two other guests besides the dog: Australian journalist/novelist, Michael Keon, and a cellist with a major Australian Symphony whose name I don't remember. My uncle was on tour, and could only join us for a couple of days. The circumstances were not the most conducive to study: the cellist was retraining his left wrist, shattered in a road accident. Keon was hiding out from a former brother-in-law, who turned out to be Philippine Dictator Ferdinand Marcos. The cellist was in agony and his intonation was off; Keon was keeping his nerves in check with considerable help from the bottle, but managed to regale us with his experiences as a newspaper correspondent covering Mao's Long March. Keon was the first literary person with whom I shared my poems, and he praised them so extravagantly that I was sure he was speaking scotch. However, when I phoned him from Perugia a couple of months later, I was told he had been flown to Washington D.C. for brain surgery! "Aha!" thought I. The story was probably only meant to throw off his real or imagined pursuers, but it was the last I ever heard of him until I read in Wikipedia that he died in 2006, aged 87. I lost contact with the cellist, but believe he recovered his intonation and his chair at the Symphony. Funny how a dog can unite such a motley group of people, each of whom was deeply absorbed in his own problems!

Ten days was Algernon with us,
behaving well, making no fuss,
giving us his rump to scratch,
with head turned round so he could watch.

He did not beg during our meals
(except with shy and mute appeals),
or whine and bark to be let out,
or wander from our whereabout.
Of course, a dog is not a saint,
but Al gave cause for small complaint.
And now he's dead. He's been put down.
His owners, back from out of town.
It seems, when he was just a tyke,
Some teddy on a motorbike
kicked at him with booted heels
and left him with a fear of wheels.
So when Rosario motored in,
Algie got scared and bit his shin.
Not badly, now, although it bled —
the dog had been vaccinated,
Rosario'd had his tetanus,
his father did not threaten us,
or them, the owners, with a lawsuit
(they bought new trouser's for Rosà's suit).
It might have ended with a raw shin
and, henceforth, a little caution —
there is such a thing as a muzzle!
To us, the whole thing was a puzzle:
they'd had the dog for several years!
But being responsible life peers,
they said he'd done this twice in past,
and so they had poor Algie gassed.

Old Black Man at the Pet Store (1976)

A found poem from Farmer's Market, in Los Angeles. He was flirting with a big parrot, and noticed that I was watching him.

You tink I'm gonna buy dis bird?
You tink I'm gonna buy dis bird?
I ain't gonna buy dis bird!
I *had* a bird!
An' he said hello when I go out
and goobye when I come home! Ha Ha!
Nah, I ain't gonna buy dis bird!

Exercise (Maybe 1981, during my first year in law school)

I wrote the following, literally as an exercise, without any serious literary or metaphysical intent. However, the title fits, doesn't it?

The harvests gathered in by sleep
bring forth new crops for him to reap;
but nought groweth again where death
hath cut his sweeping swathe.

Liveth sleep from hand to mouth;
yet, though he beggeth, all endoweth!
Death is loath a hand to lend —
except quite at the end.

Doth sleep take more than be his share?
Yet never is his cupboard bare!
Forever gorging in thy lust,
thine holdeth merely dust.

Thou'st infinite decades to feed
on thy own stinginess and greed!
Why, Death, why preyest thou on me,
when I have lived but three?

Oh Death! Couldst thou but learn from sleep —
so welcome, generous, and deep —
to secret life but not it sever,
I'd gladly sleep forever!

BLDGS (1979?)

Nothing about these new highrise
stonehenges scrapes the skies
or yearns to escape from their material
ball and chain into the ethereal
or by their sheer dimension tricks
the mind's eye into baking bricks
though they do seem to be clutching at straws
with their tremendous, concrete claws.

Nor do their upper storeys
whisper of concealed glories
or sing or cuss the omitted vowels
stifled within their abysmal bowels
but mutely brutely blankly frankly stare
at nothing across the aqueous air
abstractly measuring the middle space
with featureless, impassive face.
And yet, the optically stolid
simplicity of Coptic solids
translated from a toddler's table
makes each autistic edifice
not sphinx but angst-filled Oedipus
mulling the riddle if not the fable
What hath two legs and is condemned to dwell
in heaven the while confined to hell?

Bead Game (late 1970s)

Listening to my father, OHS, practising Beethoven's Hammerklavier Sonata, I was struck by the triumphal laughter conveyed by the opening chords. I formed a mental connection between those chords and the "sacred laughter" described in an Amerindian myth related by Claude Lévi-Strauss in Le Cru et le Cuit (Mythe No. 20, Bororo). It is the same laughter that was uttered by Archimedes when he discovered the water-displacement test for the purity of Hiero's golden crown. It is called "sacred laughter", or "laughter of the soul" because the soul who is moved to laugh in that way stands divested of all material impediments, naked as the tribesman searching the river bottom, or as Archimedes, as he ran through the streets of Syracuse shouting "Heureka! Heureka!" The Bead Game alluded to is the technique of structural association described by Hermann Hesse in his novel of that name, by which technique structural relations may be correlated among seemingly disparate entities in such a way as to produce, through a creative act, a new entity. There was also a long-standing myth that Beethoven composed the Hammerklavier Sonata to celebrate the invention of the hammer-action piano (Hammerklavier in German). Whether he did so or not does not impact the importance of that invention, or detract from its influence on the conception and performance of Beethoven's piano music. And the triumphal laughter remains. All the above matters are discussed at some length in my novel, The Carnevalis of Eusebius Asch.

Sacred laughter! Laughter of the soul!
At last the waters clear around the stone
whose point can pierce the broken shards of One
that I may make a necklace of the whole!

For shimmering through the tranquil depths of thought
appears before my probing eyes the key,
the magic key that I have always sought
by which all doors are opened up to me!

Creation dwarfs my puny, laughing speck,
but I shall seize the cosmos by its parts
and work them into one by all the arts
and wear the universe around my neck!

The *Bead Game* is but language crystal clear!
Heureka! My long-sought *Hammerklavier!*

Pygmalion (1975?)

You reinvented something called a smile,
and gave your final touches to the gaze,
and shaping and reshaping the embrace,
made love, wrought plans, and fashioned dreams awhile.

But like the poet, born to turn a phrase
and fail the word; as artists' hands, agile
in marble or in clay, themselves defile,
bringing stone to life, their own lives to disgrace,

so now you leave the work of your own tools
to live as separate as your artwork lives
within its pulsing, newly quickened clay.

Your art made lovers of two feckless fools:
one rants and raves and weeps and storms and strives,
and, now the other breathes, just walks away.

Mit Diesem Kuss (1975?)

Thou heardst my music as the flower might
while I made music out of thought and word
and of thyself a metaphor as blurred
as wings of bees in meditated flight.

As earnestly as gentle bees alight
on budding blossoms who have not yet heard
my whisperings, so briefly have I stirred
in the corolla of thine ear's delight.

And yet, what is this song that thou mayst hear?
Though waked by my disconsolate honeying,
this ecstasy I wrest from thy own ear,

resolved to steal some sweetness on the wing.
My drop of honey is a bitter tear
o'erburdened with thy nectar and my sting.

NON EXPLICIT PAUSA EST

Poetry My *Ars* (1986 or '87? Previously published in *Twilight with Halfmoon Rising*.)

> ". . . Who clipped the lion's wings
> and flea'd his rump and pared his claws?"
>
> ~T.S. Eliot

The allusions to Eliot derive from his poem, "Burbank with a Baedeker, Bleistein with a cigar." For moral as well as artistic reasons, I could not invoke the authority of this gifted antisemite without an accounting of that despicable poem. In selecting from it the motto of this satire, I was mindful of the irony in Eliot's apparent nostalgia for a Venice in which the principal enclave of moral dignity (had he only paused to think about it) would have been the Jewish Ghetto.

    Famous last words: "I want to say one thing . . ."
and out pours an interminable spring!

The last raindrops . . . presaging the deluge!
Wise men hear rumbling and take to their refuge.

I want to say one thing, but before I've said it,
shall have said more; and well your ears might dread it!

For another pair of loins girds up to dispense
the Muse like a rank tomcat on the back fence

of literature: If not for academia,
many fish were dead of writer's thalassemia

who today swim big in small ponds with one animus.
They know that publishing is not synonymous,

perforce, with everything that reeks of quality,
being closely intertwined with politics and polity . . .

    But here, Tom's pusscat, with more politesse
than most bards, and with a whit more success,

signifies her sentiments by demurring
to paper and pen, Selectrically purring

periods of protest, by punctuation
endeavoring to curtail my occupation.

    And that, I can't — though I may briefly pause
to stroke the back of some more pressing cause.

    For thus to compose verse is purest freedom.
All words herein were slaves before I freed 'em;

and I, the prisoner of my private thought,
freed by my pen . . . though some might ask, for what?

To reach outside myself for the average Joes
I cannot reach with living speech or prose?

    If so, then 'tis immoral to publish words
whose tongues have all been rooted out by surds,

or lick the unsubtle saltlicks of the ordinary
for cityfolk afoot in woods extraordinary.

Such publishing condemns my soul to prison,
fresh from the tomb of mortal mind arisen.

    Of what am I accused? What is the crime
with which I'm charged? Have I indulged in rhyme?

Or else: committed couplets? Iambic sin?
The seat of inspiration's pants worn thin,

so leaving me indecently exposed?
Or worse, with the preceding juxtaposed,

have I irreverently exposed the pose
of whimperers in emperors' new clothes?

    Who is the Felonious Arbiter, the Blackwell
whose poetic pot, calling my kettle black, will

purge my aberrant prose and strip my rogue
verse from the varicose pages of their *Vogue*?

What new precepts now govern and define
the *stesura* and *misura* of the line,

so that the kiwi flies while the eagle struts
the streets, pecking discarded scraps and butts?

Homer, although tradition has him blind,
and modern criticism, twinned or trined,

clearly discerned between words winged and wingless;
while e'en Herodas, who wrote mimes on stringless

lyres, still knew how far a flea could jump,
and the length between a lion's mane and rump.

But such distinctions, it is said, eroded
with the class barriers they once encoded:

"*Don't give us with your elegies and sonnets
your kingless crowns, your headless bourgeois bonnets!*

*Give us poems simple and real — not for the masses,
but the humanness which each of us amasses*

*in his own soul, with reverence, 'gainst all odds
in a world bereft of order, sense, or gods.*"

It takes no monumental Blackstone's *Commentary*.
to guide us to the shrine where weeping women tarry,

anointing with their tears your manifesto:
"*Qui manibus hunc locum sacer esto . . .* *

"Let this piece of earth be set apart.
Here, amid the general holocaust, lies art —

alias poetry — dead, yet alive,
suckled by wolves, yet gentle in the hive:

of this Romulean tomb, on pain of death,
do not disturb the dust with thy foul breath!"

Stand guard over that tomb and soil the plot!
Proclaim yourselves, Lagado, Camelot!

Turn up your nose at my Infernal *Canti*,
affecting umbrage at my miming Dante!

Deny estrangement from your own library,
where you've ne'er pulled the file on Alighieri,

* *Conjectural reading of the inscription on the Roman Lapis Niger.*

thumbed through the section labeled *Translatores,
Commentatores et Imitatores*;

or dined on Dante's cornucopious corpse
with other worms and maggots, to the warps!

For you bigots and pedants cannot figment
that Greek marble can have been smeared with pigment,

or tolerate that a piece of sacred bone
be crushed with profane blood on live inkstone.

   Yet I don't hear you crying, "Culture in jeopardy!"
when *La Sera del Dí di Festa* of Leopardi

becomes, in the untutored hands of (nameless)
The Evening of the Birthday Party, and, shameless,

he renders the phrase, *O donna mia*, "Jules,"
or updates the moon by throwing its pallid gules

not on the orchard rows, but rows of cars!
   But enough of idiocy, and back to *ars*:

Some think that poetry is drunken prose,
and that the poet is ready to compose

when images begin to rear and prance
like a herd of hemorrhoidal elephants.

In fact, the first thing about the whole mystique
of being a poet of the collegiate clique

is: reach for a metaphor as for a gun!
Only, don't shoot to kill, but just to stun;

and while the reader's stunned, you stick it to him!
Mikehammer it up there! Shove in your poem!

And with that insignificant suppository,
make your reader the mystified repository

of your confusion. Same should be reflected
in every line and limb, duly disjected

and strewn about, so every grisly page
looks like a scene of homicidal rage.

   If logic and horse sense evade your discourse,
relax. Sit back. Let the reader rub his whiskers.

Why should the poet do all the dirty work?
Down every tortuous alley, answers lurk

like thugs, ready to cut the reader's throat.
One of them will, no matter how remote.

Or, if not, the victim will transcend the mind —
see things to which mere intellect is blind.

Obligingly, another poet-reviewer
critiques the first in terms no less obscure,

and, choosing not to disembowel a chum,
lamely laments "what poetry has become."

But since the point is moot (and rather sore!),
leave it at that. And why flog a dead whore?

   Then, lest the air you breathe prove somewhat rare,
like a fart loosed in a minute's silent prayer,

pronounce a feeble, an execrable pun —
a pun so bad, that Attila the Hun . . .

No! A pun fit for the crossswordpuzzling Dane
nosing the stench of his lecherdomain!

For instance: "What have you been doing philately?"
queried offhandedly and intimately

of an owl engraved upon a postage stamp
(stuck on an envelope addressed from camp?).

   Or, if inspiration altogether fail,
just quote yourself on a convergent scale —

thus: "In my poem entitled *Blanketyblank*,
I wrote: . . ." and redeposit in the bank

the check you cashed on overdrawn account —
like the proverbial horse that tried to mount

itself, but never got much past the stirrup.
   Ah, poetry! My *ars*! That's still to clear up:

Poetry is that art (of lion or flea)
which summons all of speech to serve the idea.

Its fundamental unit is the verse —
its sole distinction from (at its most terse)

mere prose. It may be long or short or broken
into shards too jagged to be spoken —

provided that thus chopped it still bears scrutiny
of brain and heart, and not witness to mutiny!

  Inside that cosmic string we call the verse
(just as inside our macro-universe

of time and space lie furled micro-dimensions)
in embryo lies the *melos* Plato mentions

as logically bound to words and rhythm
(a concept that few poets have taken with 'em!)

making our unsung poetry pre-musical
in much the same way that, in wordless music, all

depends prelingual on the infant ear.
That inchoate song! May it ring out loud and clear!

  But poems can never be better than the thought —
however exquisitely the poem be wrought.

To commit to verse the commonplace, the random,
the banal and bizarre riding in tandem,

to weld loose scraps into a pile of trash is
acetylene's, not inspiration's flash, is

to defile free speech with lechery and sodomy
under the purblind aegis of the Academy —

whose members seem to share a vested interest
in inertia, alienation and disinterest!

Indeed, why risk one's job or one's alliances
to take a stand or utter swell defiances?

Why indict the murderer when it is enough
to decry murder, guns and other stuff?

Easy enough to quash the righteous urge
with a mournful tune and a Humpty-Dumpty dirge.

   Confessionals: likewise, do not confess
the whole if you can get away with less!

In that regard, sex invariably serves
to exit the entrée via the hors d'oeuvres.

There are more things in heaven and earth, Horatio,
than are dreamt of in your poem on fellatio . . .

Depict raw Sapphic foreplay in the sand,
and people think you bare your soul and hand!

Meanwhile, the bashful ace creeps up the sleeve.
Good Lord! If poems allowed us to perceive

those hidden cards, at least we'd recognize
a fellow being shuffling a pack of lies!

   All that aside, a poet must still conform
to the image which puts him outside the norm.

Not, God forbid, a Titan with concentric
rings, but Joe *Unaveraged*, mildly eccentric,

sprawled out upon a lake beneath the moon,
in a leaky rowboat, drunk as a baboon.

Or: *shed your togs to interpolate a beaver*!
And similar long passes to a wide receiver.

   While thus fleeing from the literary sauna
into an ice-cold bath of flora and fauna,

do not neglect to list each woodsy species
peopling your *opera omnia's* leafy niches,

and introduce yourself as an ombudsman
of Academe to American backwoodsmen.

    And lastly, with your milkweed and your plovers
now firmly pressed between your country covers,

make sure that one of them displays your portrait —
the writer's humble bow to visual *Vortritt*:

The Poet In Reflective Shades and Leather.
Tough guy. Yet shy. Fresh-landed from the ether.

Or else, a candid shot, domestic locus,
in a 'Sixties' unposed pose, just out of focus.

    The best of you write poems polished, cerebral,
allusive and alluvial, a little febrile,

about dreams given up to join the system,
how youth's messiahs knocked, and how you missed 'em;

how nothing can express the inexpressible
effect of silence being turned up a decibel . . .

*Do such give you the right to see dissent
buried beneath a pile of excrement?*

    Then don't chastise the lowly, famished worm
for being true to itself in mien and form.

For even obsequious Mr. Eliot
(who deigned to inject the Jew beneath the lot

and wondered, were the Jews of Venice cause
of her decline and of the Seven Laws'?)

did not forbear to season the sublime
with ample use of assonance and rhyme,

and firmly drove among the rats and piles
iambic verse to prop contemporary styles.

One thing to oppose nostalgia and reaction;
another, by presumption and by faction,

to throttle the big speech and the small press
which all, by dint of literacy, possess.

Statesmen and bards fought hard to endow their brothers
with freedoms you now use to silence others.

If guarding Dante's tomb you seek asylum,
surely you revere not, only revile him.

Such posturing must turn your Athenaeum
into a cesspool or a mausoleum.

   Many before me, similarly affected,
have toiled to see that Poet resurrected.

Too often have the graves of greats been breached
by them to let the living be impeached

instead. And once — so says a well-loved script —
emerging from his urine-spattered crypt

to berate the scads of bibulous night visitors
and the hypocrisy of bigots and inquisitors,

Alighieri's ghost spoke words supremely apt
to leave this treatise neatly tied and wrapped:

   "If anyone speak ill of me, or bull,
t'ai è da di' ch'a veg a bug' d'e' cul!" *

   * *Una Notte di Dante*, in Olindo Guerrini, *Sonnetti Romagnoli* (Bologna, 1920), p. 197.

A Silvia (late 1970s?) Giacomo Leopardi

Sylvia, do you remember still
those days departed of your mortal life
when beauty shone so radiant
in your laughing and averted eyes
and blissful in your thoughts you scaled the rim
the very rim of youth?

   The tacit rooms resounded
and the encircling ways
with your perpetual song
while you, absorbed upon your womanly tasks,
would sit so well content
to clasp the inchoate future in your mind.
It was sweet-smelling May, and you were wont
thus to spend your days.

   I, the congenial studies
oft forsaking, and the perspired page
on which my earliest age
and of myself the worthier part were squandered,
bent o'er the porch of the paternal homestead
would turn my ears toward the sound of your voice
and to the fleeting hands
that fretted to and fro' the tedious cloth.
I'd scan the untroubled sky,
the gilded paths and the orchard rows
and thence the sea from afar, and then the hills.
Mortal tongue can't say
what I felt inside.

   What gentle thoughts we thought,
what hopes, what hearts, O Sylvia mine!
What conception we then had
of human life and fortune!
When I hark back to so much hopefulness
an oppression o'ertakes me
disconsolate and sharp
and I return to ache of my affliction.

O nature! O nature!
Why do you not surrender
what once you promise? Why of so great store
do you defraud your young?

   You, before the summer could parch the grass,
by a hidden ill waylaid and overwhelmed
perished tenderling. Neither set you eyes
on the flower of your years.
Nor was your heart to be wooed
by the sweet praises of your long black hair
or of sidelong and love-struck glances.
With you, the handmaids of your votive days
would never converse of love.

   Thereafter perished quickly
also my sweet dreams, and to my years
as well the fates denied
their rightful youth.
Ay passed, how art thou passed
dear companion of my innocence,
all my banished hope!

   Is this that world? Are these
the joys, the love, the endeavors, the adventures
we spoke so solemnly and often of?
Is this the state allotted to mankind?
At the first glimmer of truth,
O miserable, you fell. And with your hand
to cold death and an unadornèd tomb
pointed me the way.

On the Interpretation of Beethoven in the Late Twentieth Century (early to mid-1980s). Previously published in *Twilight with Halfmoon Rising*.

    In reverberant rhombuses of sombre walls
of cunningly constructed concert halls,
or beneath the stars, in bowls carved from the hills,
like Pelean tongues poured from volcanic stills
does the music die an animal enraged
at thus being born acoustically encaged?
Or, like the pelted pond or taut plucked string,
does it fade from being, vanishing ring by ring?
    Swims Beethoven inside our atmosphere,
perched on the heads of jostling molecules
like waterbearing slaves, to be splashed in pools
for the casual pleasure of the pilgrim's ear?
    He had a soberer conception of his task
than to fill the ephemeral, Sisyphean flask
of power and fame. Nor did the artist cower
within art's ivory, himself a moral, tower.
    No one disputes this man intended more
than to dip the frozen grasp of his blasted ears
into the boundless music of the spheres
and tip the closecupped grains into the score.
    Versed in the major issues of his time,
whether practical or imbued with the sublime,
whether weaving the perfection of Penelopeia
or unraveling his Homeric melopoeia
(all the while o'erwhelmed by the insidious wooing
of music in its most mindful manifestations),
whether scrawling or expunging dedications,
the composer knew exactly what he was doing . . .
    Which is not to say devotion never faulted him:
The interstitial songs which so exalted him
as their most disposed and sympathetic scribe
he rendered faithfully in a vernacular
revered as ageless, awesome and spectacular.

It's just that the motivation doesn't jibe . . .
Not to imply the man is overrated (!)
but that such pretentions now seem somewhat dated.
We can appreciate, the craft, the logic,
the intellect, without the anagogic.
So spare us, please, the posturing and the preaching,
the ecstatic swells, the expanding and up-reaching!
Spare us anything profound or seminal
or vaguely philanthropic or trigeminal.
This music knows exactly where it's going,
and needs no signposts quickening or slowing.
   Why overindulge its young, Romantic pulse?
After all, is this not the Age of Consenting Adults?
Your place or mine? That is the subtle question,
figuratively speaking, which intrigues
(for it requires no chanticleered suggestion!)
the modern public. Anything more fatigues.
Precision, power, control, "lush carpets of sound." *
That is what makes the compact disc go round.
Genius survives in art. The rest is dross.
Rejoice in the contemporary. Cut the loss.

   "Durch alle Toene . . . ein leiser Ton gezogen!"

   Through all these tones, a fainter tone emerges,
home from the War, purged of the recent purges,
echoing with the insistence of a slogan,
crosses the stage, electrically mounts the podium,
irradiates us with an unsuspected odium,
engulfs the orchestra, *siegheils*, and vaunts,
"We are a Volk that knows just what it wants . . ."
   The resurrected specter of Doctor Goebbels,
foiled by the fact of Furtwaengler, now ennobles
the scene in tails, for a sentimental token,
his rope now tied a bow where the neck was broken.**
Shall not he preside over the humble *partitur*-men,
raise the baton, deliver the virile sermon,

   * *Typical phrase culled from* Time *Magazine's Music section.*
   ** Wishful thinking: he took poison.

disseminate the Word, make safe the Roster
from heretic, pretender, and impostor?
"No longer are we a Volk of art and culture . . ."
The peacock now is transformed into a vulture,
able to strip semantic meat from bone
and, chewing, proclaim in Orwellian undertone,
"Peace is war; love, hate; and freedom, slavery;
Beethoven, bombast; and honor, knavery."
For birds in name, though feathered to the marrow,
when predators, can ill afford one sparrow.

"Freunde! Nicht diese Töne!" Not these tones!

The *Ode to Joy* is no military march,
and not by rearing a pompous marble arch,
not by fanfare of trumpets and trombones
is such a man appropriately remembered.
Nor, morally disemboweled, deveined, dismembered,
will his work be reconciled to an empty dome
by manly *geste* or commercial metronome.
Approach his music not without demands
that its prime exponents, cleansed of all profanity,
bear witness to, and compassion for humanity
no less, nor less impassioned, than the man's.
For I can't see him chandeliered with tin,
the media's faithful friend and constant focus,
Culture's Diplomat - or diplodocus,
squandering David's praise on Gunga Din;
since, admirable as sometimes such things are,
the man was neither celebrity nor star.
And if we can't perceive that inner tone
which so transcends the earthly treble clef,
hearing naught but that to which the man grew deaf,
then it will be asked, Whose ear was truly stone?
and whether such deafness marks not well the grave
of what he was and, through his music, gave.

Each in His Own Way (circa 1981; revised June 19, 2017)
For David and Diane Swenson

We had all read some version of the pome
in which the poet found one upturned butterfly
in Shakespearian throes, and took it home
to see it revive or, summoning one last flutter, die.

Yet there he lay, half-dead — worse: on the beach,
where roiling ranks of waves unleashed invade
the shore and rush headlong into the breach
just as the *deus ex* arrives in aid.

But gently in hand, now rinsed of salt and foam
fanning his monarch wings, yellow as butter, dry,
he gave no song of praise, no grateful speech;
we heard no violins, no serenade;

yet we all gasped as he took wing and soared,
each murmuring private thanks unto the Lord.

The Question (1982). Previously published in *Twilight*.

I asked my Zaydeleh, a saintly man,
Reb Szulim Reder, in his black caftan,

"Zaydeleh," I said, "I am perplexed,
and cannot find my guide in any text.

From the day the sun began once more to shine
upon a Jewish land in Palestine,

we Jews have not been object of less hate,
now that we constitute a Jewish State;

nor are we therefore less subject to libel
because that State is founded on the Bible.

But being so based (if not in fact, in principle),
and having proved, against all odds, invincible,

are we not by our own successes bound
in a new Covenant on historic ground?

And if that's true, and if this Pact were broken
(may God forbid, and such words not be spoken!)

then does this State of ours have right to life
when its existence causes so much strife?

It seems that so much turmoil around one nation
calls for a little more justification,

since history, Holocaust, despair and doubt
have shown the world we could survive without?"

    Profound silence followed while Zayde listened —
long after I'd finished speaking. His eyes glistened.

At last, he spoke, and this is what he said,
(for I still hear his words inside my head):

    "If one could somehow leaven bread with questions,
or raise up tabernacles with suggestions,

there would be neither Pesach nor matzot,
and only the suggestion of Sukkot.

But since we're seated round the Shabbes table . . .
My Zayde once told me a little fable:

    "Once upon a time, there was a shtetl . . .
But I began my story in the middle:

The Emperor owed a favor to the Jews.
So he decreed (and no one could refuse!)

that they should build the famous town of Chelm,
and build it in the middle of his Realm,

amid the Cossacks, Turks and Poles and Prussians,
the Tatars and the Huns, the Serbs and Russians.

They built. Chelm grew, and soon approached perfection
beneath the Emperor's benign protection.

"But as the Potentate increased in years,
so too increased his troubles and his fears.

Sist du, the Kaiser was afraid of dying.
And so, the *priesters*, after years of trying

to detach the Jews from his paternal knee,
made him revoke, for penance, the Decree!

"Thus Chelm ceased to exist, and all therein;
ceased to exist! To purge the Imperial Sin!

Chelm and all its codes and codicils,
its records, deeds and debts, its trusts and wills.

Ceased in an instant! Throughout the realm,
no lips dared form the stricken name of   .

As if by bureaucratic thunderclap,
the town of Chelm vanished from every map.

"Now Chelm itself went on much as before;
naches and *tzuris*, neither less nor more.

Still went to shul, still *davened*, danced and cried,
still cooked for Shabbes, still matched groom and bride.

Still plied a bustling trade with neighboring towns,
still dealt in coin, lent funds to bankrupt crowns.

In short, Chelm was the same *gefilte fishl* —
except now, everything was . . . unofficial!

"In a way, this was a *mechayeh* for the Jews:
the priests could not denounce them to the pews;

the lawyers could no longer bring false suit
on them — for if they did, the case was moot!

No court could sentence them to death or time —
the law said 'Chelmers' could commit no crime!

And so, *sine jure, sine delicto*,
they existed — not *de facto*, but *de ficto*!

For *doktor, shoychet, moyhel* kept their praxes,
and, at year's end, found out there were no taxes!

   "Of course, not everything was hunky dory.
There is another side to Zayde's story:

Whenever Jews were beaten, robbed or burned,
it was a deaf ear that the Emperor turned.

For good or evil, in their dereliction,
the Chelmer Jews were now so much a fiction,

the great Descartes took note of their denial,
and wrote: 'I am, because you have my file!'

   "And then, somehow it started that whenever
someone did something on review not clever,

or something suddenly just 'disappeared,'
or some Ambassador singed the Emperor's beard,

or Anarchists were found to have conspired
against the Throne, or something worse transpired —

terrible things, too terrible to name! —
then, naturally, whom do you think they'd blame?

Of course! Who else? They blamed the Chelmer Jews —
In signs and whispers, first; then, in the News.

   "So Chelm became — forgive me — an abyss,
down which all worldly filth poured with the hiss

of libel, slander, lies and defamation,
perjury, innuendo, and denigration.

"Until the world did something so immense,
so horrible, depraved, devoid of sense,

that even Chelm could not be blamed or framed —
if from the ashes Chelm could be reclaimed . . . !

"And so, *mein bub*, I answer with a question:
Suppose that on a similar 'suggestion,'

the Nations all went back upon their word,
and of this Jewish State no more were heard:

What lies, what filth, what dirt, what excrement
would the world's peoples now have to invent,

if all the garbage which they once hurled down
on Chelm, they could have hurled at *one small town?*"

Apologia (1988 or '89). Previously published in *Twilight*.

If I had not been traveling from Rome to Los Angeles immediately after the massacre, I would not have seen the huge discrepancies between US and European coverage of the event. It was immediately apparent that US news media — print and broadcast — were acting in concert with government directives; whereas, as emerged from my later research, French, German, Italian and English press, though working independently, were reporting figures 20 and 30 times higher.

On September 8, 1978,
a day that every bereaved son and daughter
of King Cyrus, to us known as "the Great",
remember as Black Friday, day of slaughter,

the late usurper of the Peacock Throne,
irked by the masses gathering in protest,
ordered his sycophants to shoot them down:
men, women, children, babes clutching the breast.

And our Free Press, steeped in the holy water
of the First Amendment, rose as one
to conceal the facts from the unsteadfast West,
and of three thousand dead tolled ninety-eight!

Did not humanity demand an answer?
Yet none would talk. For that, I sued the censor. *

> *See Gimpel v. ABC, CBS & NBC, 3 FCC Records (No. 15) 4575 (1988). I lost the case because I had not submitted "extrinsic evidence"— *which the Commission defined as insider testimony. Go figure!*

Dim Star (1986?). Previously published in *Twilight*.

If I were prisoner of an impious kingdom,
eclipsed by trials as utterly lost as noble,
begging for scraps, which my imprisoners fling to me
with hearts immovable and minds immobile,

I could not treasure more the blessed sight of you
through the precious cracks in my obscure existence
in which I twist and turn like a bat in the night of youth
sensing, without encountering, the resistance

of inexorable decrees. Just sing to me, sing to me,
little bird, high, high on the barred sill of global
darkness, the blue of space in the eyes' distance
and the dim star that, just to the right of you,

threads my unravelling soul with the love and light of you
that must remain the prize, privilege and right of youth . . .

The Legacy (1986) Previously published in *Plains Poetry Journal*, vol. 28 (1989), p. 15.

Dryops lay dying, a curled and smoking cinder
of his great literary conflagration —
an offering of erotic inspiration
of which the world needs no obtuse reminder —

and all but blind, and lame, and weak of bladder,
he summoned to his side his last big flame,
whose merit was, his eros, still not tame,
made one last lunge at life (but never had her!)

that he might gently, tactfully remind her
of his letters, and, calling her by name,
asked her intentions re their publication,
and bade her do with them as her heart bade her.

Thus spoke the generous heart of the dying satyr.
And the lady's heart, she said, bade, "*Imprimatur!*"

Portent (date unknown; previously published in *Twilight with Halfmoon Rising*.)

One heatwave summer evening at the zoo,
a peacock rose in flames from the bush, with triad
trumpetcall flew over the amazed, myriad
gaping throng, and like a manitou

atop a totem pole, spreading fans of blue,
lighted upon a youth's blond, curls-awry head;
and he, parrying the stroke of swift, hendyad
shock and dread, amid the hullabaloo,

finding all eyes upon him, commenced to clown,
heedless of those upon him gazing down
from aperch his own disheveled, bleeding crown.

And so it is with those their own fame awes.
They feel the weight, they suffer the sharp claws —
yet presume to dance to alien applause!

Two Poems by Rilke

Torso (late 1980s). Previously published in *Twilight With Halfmoon Rising*

Although Rilke entitled this sonnet "Archaic Torso of Apollo", there is nothing archaic about the torso he describes. On the contrary, the description matches strikingly the famous black, basalt torso in the Uffizi, from a copy of the lost bronze Doryphoros by the classical sculptor Polykleitos. The Post-Romantic poets had tired of the Romantic obsession with Classical Greece, and sought their artistic ideals in the postulated raw spontaneity of Greek sculptors of the Archaic Period. This spectacular sonnet of Rilke's remains, notwithstanding, distinctly classical in inspiration.

We were not liege to know the astounding head
in which his apple eyes grew ripe and round;
but in his torso soft lights still abound,
holding gleams of his aspect — dimmed, not dead.

Else could the ship's prow of his chest not blind,
and in the faint curve of his gentle loins
a smile not linger where it softly joins
the memory of procreant mankind.

Else would this stand mere stone, deformed and halt
beneath the ruin of an ethereal shoulder,
and not glisten so, like a wild beast's pelt,

nor burst from every surface with its rays
like a star. No part but lays bare the beholder,
you cannot hide: you have to change your ways!

The Apple Garden (2007)

A friend sent me Seamus Heaney's translation of this little masterpiece, and finding it incoherent and specious, I resolved to do better. The inspiration and structural development of the original are very clear, very poignant, and impossible to translate unless one understands that the poet portrays himself here as working his way through a succession of tentative comparisons, to express by visual simile an inner feeling that he finds impossible to describe in words. Hence the successive "als . . . wie . . . wie. . . ."

When a poem adopts this "groping" attitude, the imposition of rhyme contradicts the intended uncertainty, as the verses may appear to do the bidding of the rhyme, rather than its internal reason. It is a token of Rilke's mastery that he avoids this danger—in part through the weak rhymes "die" and "wie" in the third stanza.

It is also worth noting that among the several hundred reproductions of woodcuts, etchings, drawings and paintings of Albrecht Dürer that I have searched in print and on line, not one have I found that portrays apple trees as such. I did find three woodcuts ("Knight Trooper", "Adam and Eve", and "The Fall"), each showing a fruit tree in the background – plausibly apples. These fruits hang sparse and light—a far cry from Rilke's description of swollen pomes and bending boughs. Rilke's probable invention of "Dürer's trees" is consistent with his poetic of transforming thought, feeling and imagination into visual, plastic image. Compare Rilke's transformation of classical into "archaic", in the sonnet, "Torso", above.

Come quickly thou, now that the sun has set,
and see the sky turn green upon the close!
Is it not as though we'd long been gathering this
and laying it up in store inside ourselves

for just this moment – from old memories
new hope and half-forgotten happiness
(not free from inner darkness!) to distill
in thought and strew therewith the ground before us?

As if, beneath the boughs of Dürer's trees
that bear the weight of a hundred days of toil
in the overfullness of their bursting fruit,
devoted still, enduring, still endeavouring . . .

as if something still remained beyond all bearing
to be heaved and hefted up and offered whole –
if one can stand prepared one's whole life long
to want One Thing Only, and grow, and hold one's peace!

He Who Has Art (late 1980s or early 1990s)

> *Wer Wissenschaft und Kunst besitzt*
> > *hat auch Religion;*
>
> *Wer jene beiden nicht besitzt*
> > *Der habe Religion!*
>
> *He who art and science owns*
> > *religion also hath;*
>
> *He who neither of them owns,*
> > *religion be his path!*
>
> > — Goethe

Lord God of song, where would I find the voice
to uplift my thoughts thus in faint-hearted prayer,
if not for art, which makes my soul rejoice
when Thy remoteness makes my heart despair?

If downward leans the heart to the wild beasts' lair,
yet may it seek refuge in the quiet cloister
of ordered chaos and abstracted care —
if the will can be inclined to make that choice.

Yet rather is it art's mysterious power
to quell the storms, dispel the dense confusion
which so distract in one's tormented hour.

Neither the world's mirror, nor an illusion,
art speaks for itself, inviting Thy steps lower,
that wandering souls not suffer Thy exclusion.

March 12, 1989 (date unknown)

Time pinched out the bright flame at last
and burnt its fingers . . .

Allegory (1988 or '89) Previously published in *Twilight With Halfmoon Rising.*

God pricked Himself.
Out bled the world.
A droplet.
A tiny globe which welled up round and red
and rolled from the divine Finger into nothingness.
whose sole property was to magnify
the least thing not itself
into a universe.
This was an accident.
For He was sewing the garments for the souls
of all things living
when the divine Hand trembled.
In seven days He made the world.
Days before days.
But that first moment —
the pinprick in space and time —
that was the work of man,
whose coming trials made shake the hand of God.

Prophecy (date unknown; I revised it many times.)
Tommaso Campanella (1568 - 1639)

Darkness all around! Most of us drowsed,
drugged with ignorance. And hired strings
provided song for infamous repose.
Others, watchful, robbed us of our things
(honor and blood!) or forced themselves, aroused,
on either sex and shamed the comatose!
I lit a light! There! Startled, vermin rose
in swarms. Banished the dark, fautrix of schemes,
from before our eyes! Avenged, robbers and rogues!
On the dimwits, on the demagogues
the bestial contents of their ruptured dreams!
The sheep allied themselves with wolves in trust
against the valiant dogs.
Both ended prey to their own greed and lust!

Syllogism (1988 or '89)

Who suffers? Nature? Flowers thrive or wilt,
and blossoms burst upon the thriving plant
beside the sick and manifest no guilt.
Insects can feel, but aren't much more gallant:

The mantis mates and eats her lover's head!
Warm fur would seem to have respect for pain,
since mammals nurse their young and mourn their dead.
Yet for compassion one must search in vain

till man; and he, immersed unto the hilt
in tragedy and farce, excess and want,
inflicts or suffers tyranny and dread,
yet neither will nor can therefrom refrain.

Agreed: somewhere the universe is flawed;
but he who suffers most is plainly God!

Rebuttal (1988 or '89)

Of course, such reasoning would not apply
if God, in fact, were like the common fly.

What leads me now to so hypothesize
is something in the segments of the eyes.

For God's view of the world must be composite
to suffer so much suffering—if not cause it!

The Book (1981). After Giovanni Pascoli (1855 – 1912).
Previously published in *Twilight with Halfmoon Rising*.

In a corner of the alcove was a book,
lying open on a lectern of old oak.

Outside, the wind. The aged oakstand dreamed
of murmuring woods. The open volume seemed

to be listening to the woodworm softly working.
And I felt a presence, as of something lurking . . .

It came not by the door, where the drafts do battle
with hinge and latch, making them creak and rattle

(capricious gusts!), but it was there, was slowly —
hear the rustling? — riffling through the *folii!*

I cannot see, but hear and am aware
of a thing invisible as thought or air.

Someone stands there, leafing through the pages —
from first to last, and then — it seemed like ages —

leafing from the last leaf to the first.
The search is fruitless. With impulsive burst,

by twenties, thirties, a hundred at once, he fans
the fragile pages with impatient hands.

Now hesitating, one by one he curls them.
Now, in a tantrum, page upon page he hurls them.

But wait! He stops! Has he found what he was seeking?
All is still. The door has ceased its creaking.

Does he read? But briefly . . . then, as if consumed,
he bends anew the page, his search resumed.

And evening finds him still shuffling the pages.
I hear a sound like prayers of ancient Sages;

like the gentle flapping of the velvet tent
of night that by the moon still finds him bent

in vain upon his endless, hopeless quest.
And still and always I can hear my guest —

the soft crackling of parchments, as of fire
lingering, smoldering, loath to expire.

Always and still, my ears perceive the whisper,
as of wind through autumn leaves (but drier, crisper)

as he searches like a fever, like an aura,
back and forth, the pages of the Torah —

for Torah was the book. But did I heed
the message of that restless soul? Indeed,

message it was — and I say it with a sigh;
for the book was mine, and alas, the soul was I . . .

First in Thought (around 1989)

Father, Who made the world in seven days —
by the first count — and on the seventh rested,
why have You charged those who would keep Your ways
to keep the Sabbath holy, and so blessed it?

Is it because that day the whole world vested
in humankind, as the new moon's first phase,
unseen by the eye, yet tugs at the whitecrested
wave although untouched by the moon's rays?

The path to righteousness a seabed strewn
with unanswerables? For if the seas divide,
is it not because nothing is granite-hewn?

My heart dwells in darkness, yet feels the tide
of deep seas rising under a dark moon —
"as a young man rejoiceth o'er his bride."

Wrestler's Prayer (around 1989)

My God, turning to You, I dream of sin
and turning away, I feel Your all-seeing eyes,
so cannot end nor yet even begin,
the stars unmoved to either set or rise.

The head knows what is right, the heart, unwise
beyond its years, resists, the soul, stretched thin,
cries life and death and neither lives nor dies,
but both, cut off from this, her earthbound twin.

What greater punishment could You devise
than tears of fire — than fire of frigid flame?
Your clemency, Your sternness are the same.

Wrestling myself, I cannot hope to win,
pray only that this hold could make me lame,
that a man might not walk brazen into shame!

A Prayer (around 1989)

Delay, deny, dear God, my prayers, my pleas,
entreaties, *kvitels*, all on hold, on hold
all, all till when? Till, like a calf of gold,
my desire is crushed, ground up and drunk to the lees?

Wilt Thou make of Thyself my prisonhold,
that I not come and go as I well please?
Wilt Thou bring me defeated to my knees,
that I not kneel save by Thy stranglehold?

Am I a rat in laboratory maze,
that Thou shouldst goad me from deadend to end
until the end of all my wasted days?

Thou wantest me broken, though I surely bend,
that broken, every piece should sing Thy praise:
Thou leadest me out of Egypt with a strong hand . . . !

TESHUVAH (Previously published in *Twilight with Halfmoon Rising*)

1: *Oniah* (1984)

It was the hour when melancholy pales
in the west into a darkening sky,
the hour in which the navigating heart,
vexed by faithless mauve and fickle green
turns with longing to the shore;
the hour that turns the sea opaque
and bids the night "Bestir thyself!"
beneath the blanket of a sapphire lake;
the nethering hour of neither night nor day,
when night, still dreaming of a since forgotten word
and finding itself by filaments and swirls awake
gestures a hand as if to speak — and then,
remembering, lets it fall again.
It was the hour when light through light —
when teeming schools of squamous light
swim through opalescent seas of light
like galaxies colliding in the gleaming night.
It was that hour that hour that hour —
the hour of Eliot and Alighier,
of Sapphic odes, of evening prayer.
    And I, cruising the margin of the known cosmos,
glimpsed in the furtive, fleeting corner of an eye,
in the tryst of pewtered tide and crystal blue,
in the blackbody blackness of the lampblack hills
that sucked from the radar dishes of their skull
my searchlight eyes, the transitory planes —
the intersecting planes of hidden worlds —
saw them rise before my windshield,
shatter — so it seemed — and fall
in fragments on the shiny bonnet of my car
and slide and dart and as if abscond
like carp beneath the glass of an obsidian pond.
And in every sliver of those fractured dimensions,

as if in ice reflected and refracted,
my life a staring fish, frozen, protracted.
For in the silvered cockpit of that glacial fish
sat I, pervious and pregnable to each particle of light,
a whistle in the breeze, a smoke in the wind
drifting toward Malibu
blue Malibu now pointless alibi —
Point Mugu now point sans omega,
and saw with my invisible eyes
the seethrough of myself,
of all my acts and words and ideas,
of logical premise beyond assail
grown suddenly and inexplicably frail,
and saw the seethrough of the world
like an animal all unimpressed with miracles.
   So I said aloud what a man might say
when he turns transparent and his hair turns gray
and the years come out like the seldom stars
and the stars come out aglittering cold and pale,
throwing their rivery light on the moonlike sail
on the tall sharp mast of the halfmoon heart —
Ah world, I said, ah world ah world,
like a man who knows he is already dead,
your magic tricks were not enough!
I go to tremble like the universe
quaking in its quantum boots . . .

2. Day and Night (1988)

I misremembered! In Lucretius' introduction to his poem On Nature, *the poet tells Memmius to study "in placid, night-time vigil" (see above, at page 50), explaining that the terrors of death and the unknown should be dispelled, not by the light of the sun, but by reason alone. True, this requires some careful reflection. In the first place, much of the poem's instruction could only be based on daylight observation. Second, the advice was personal to Memmius, who, so the poet tells us, was of a superstitious bent and afraid of dying. Let him, therefore, befriend the night through tranquil study! Moreover, as a high government official, Memmius might have exposed himself to prosecution by pursuing in open daylight an atheist philosophy irreconcilable with the official cult of the Roman State. Nevertheless, a mistake is a mistake!*

*   Maimonides follows the Talmud, which tells us that, since one does not earn one's living during the night, "nighttime was created for studying Torah."*

Lucrece by day, Maimonides by night,
believed that learning was the most ideal,
the day being free of superstitious fright,
the night, of the illusion of being real.

Because not superstitious, I agree
with the *Rambam* that nighttime is more fitting,
if the daylight masks complexity,
and all is to be crammed into one sitting.

But on the other hand, perhaps Lucretius
wasn't wrong, if truth must stand to light.
Myself, I think that learning is most precious
when two lamplighters meet in the twilight.

And so I thought, but didn't realize
how swift dusk falls, and how it fools the eyes.

3. The Heart Knows (1988)

Knower of All Hearts, does mine believe
that You descended on Mount Sinai and gave
into Moses' hands the Law? Or do I deceive
myself and those with whom I dare to *daven*?

You are my God, because You have commanded
it so, but all Your Books cannot engrave
my heart with the sheer conviction of Your candid
signs. And yet, I too was once a slave

in Egypt, and was freed by what small learning,
what few *Mitzvot* I keep, and by the example
of holy Jews. I too am filled with yearning
for God, the Rebbe, and the Holy Temple —

and pray that You, in Your great lovingkindness,
will turn to all who grope for You in blindness.

4. Believe it or Not (1988)

Believe it or not, as a child of six or seven,
I read in Ripley's opus of awesome name
about a man who could see the stars at noon.
In his eyes, the sun did not obscure its frame

of lesser fires. He perceived in a half-light haze.
For him, 'twas always twilight — with half moon rising.
      God's eyesight must be much the same.
For Him, the stars are not obscured by the blaze

of suns. He sees all, light and dark, with even
sweep. And there's the magic of the phase:
that for a breathtaking instant, it is given
to us to see the great, blueescent balloon

of Creation which the Blessed One hath wrought
— through the Creator's eyes, *believe it or not* . . . !

5. Deposition (1990)

  same shot from a different angle
the sun was changing on the buildings
and the time it was pure night
there is no comparison to save time
I just went fairly directly
pretty much right into the night
just dissolved like
like an aesthetic decision
between the time

  there was a middle part to this
an aesthetic decision
here is left out the magic hour
piece of the between the time
left out the magic
day to night dissolved like two together
no comparison to save

   the sun was changing
right into the night
just stuck the metre out in it
did what it says
just went fairly directly
just dissolved like
from a different angle

   between the time
the sun was changing
and the time it was pure night
I just dissolved the two together
day to night like day tonight
left out the piece of the
went right into the
My thoughts are not your thoughts
two together
night pure night
do what it says

The Other Side (1989.) Previously published in *Twilight with Halfmoon Rising*.

If God is, which reason cannot decide,
we need not wonder why it is so hard
to love Him, loving from the other side
One so exalted with means so Abélard.

But let us not therefore lightly discard
that *if*: for a God in Whom all souls reside,
light of His light, unmassed, unavatared,
is not more easily loved, or less, denied.

Is fire not temperate to its scion spark?
Thus thirsting would we fall to drink our fill,
expelled from Eden, branded with His mark,

to feel what flames obscure in the blazing ark,
as though to train by practice of free will
our fiery eyes to focus on the dark!

Sweet Rice (mid-1980s) As told to me by Mr. Bin Ong.

Du Fu, old Poet, in fame steadfastly simple,
took refuge from the flood in Buddha's temple

high on a hill; and worrying how to carve
in wood his final poem, prepared to starve.

Until the faithful Prefect, having scoured
the town for food the flood had not devoured,

sent him a boat with glutinous sweet rice —
enough for several poets to suffice.

And three days hungry, never having tasted
the food of gods, Du Fu left nothing wasted.

But poets' bowels, inured to humbler fare
could not accept a luxury so rare,

could not digest what poets' tongues could savor,
grown old on gruel with dust and tears for flavor.

Thus the Poet died. And so shall I,
knowing bitterness so well, of sweetness die.

To Ben Before his Journey (mid-1980s) Previously published in *Twilight with Halfmoon Rising*. For Uncle Bin Ong.

My friend, I know, knowing whence you are descended,
you hear in you, overwhelming and orchestral,
the irrefutable cry of your ancestral
home, and the long summons leaves you suspended

in a middle kingdom (yes, pun intended!),
like the hovering hawk some call the kestrel,
like "the tree that would be calm in the mistral." *
In your speech, your vision, two worlds are blended.

    *See note at end of poem, next page.

So grieved your favorite poets (their fate entwined
with state) when called from their small patch of chaste land.
Will you find solace where your poets pined?

Alas, between surrogates and sedatives,
this place you pitched your tent is a true wasteland.
Here everyone is homesick — even the natives.

> Note: The quotation is from a poem in Mandarin by my esteemed friend, Mr.
> Bin Ong, as translated to me by himself.

Those Dancin' Feet (1987) Previously published in *Twilight with Halfmoon Rising.*)

I dreamt our country fell into the hands
of hoofers, hacks, and hypocrites and whores.
Our leaders posed and pandered to the fans.
Their policies were set to movie scores.

The people knew the whole thing was an act.
Yet all surrendered to the mass seduction,
unwilling to sort fantasy from fact
in the middle of an MGM production.

Each time another scandal popped its glans
It just blent in with the prevailing mores.
Stars ran for office. Drama schools were packed.
And Wall Street soared! For none foresaw destruction

till Broadway crashed beneath the marching soles
of all the chorus lines bound for the polls!

Politician (1987)

Dear Mr. Hart:
        I hear you're going to run again,
to toss your hat into the contenders' ring.
You say you won't indulge that kind of fun again,
and that the last time was your final fling.

Please understand: I don't care whom you sleep with,
whether Donna, Daisy Mae, or Suzy;
or give a hoot what company you keep with,
or why you're not a little bit more choosey.

What bothers me about your last shenanigan
is that at first you'd lie when caught full swing,
and jeopardize a presidential leap with
a dumb romance with a designing floozy.

Come, Mr. Hart! They'll pluck you like a fowl.
Best keep your hat, and just throw in the towel.

Dante in Disneyland: Canto VII (Previously published in *Twilight with Halfmoon Rising*.)

Sometime in the mid-1970s, I proposed, in a fit of madness, to write a grand poem in the style of the Divine Comedy satirizing the contemporary state of the world. As preposterous as that sounds, I am only one of many dozens of poets, some of them very notable, who have attempted the same thing. I completed five and one-half cantos, including this one commemorating the Challenger disaster of 1986. There is a video of me giving a rather mediocre reading of it on the occasion of the 30th anniversary of this enormous and eminently avoidable tragedy. The agonizing tale of how it was not avoided is meticulously set forth in Richard C. Cook's outstanding exposé, Challenger Revealed, NY, Thunder Mouth Press *(2006).*

My five-plus cantos of Dante in Disneyland *were not written in* terza rima *(interlocking tercets), but in pairs of enclosed tercets, symbolizing an existential dichotomy that was not meant to be resolved until the Third Canticle (Paradiso). I trust that Moshiach will come before I finish the First Canticle.*

Canto Seven begins with the actual application I mailed in to NASA, in answer to President Reagan's call for public participation in the great adventure.

"Dear Mr. President:
                        I won't be subtle:
I understand you'll take an application
for the first civilian space ride on the Shuttle

from teachers of all walks and every station.
Well, Sir, if not being hired is no rebuttal,
then I'm as good as any in the nation.

So please accept herewith my *resumé*,
my doctoral degree (now doctoroid,
being from a foreign *université!*)

and don't count off because I'm unemployed.
My reference letters are a bit passé,
but 'sweets to the sweet', so void for the void.

"I know I haven't got a schoolboy's prayer,
yet somehow I'm as sure I've found my hack
to the stars as that your Shuttle's found a fare.

"Just one more thing, before I start to pack:
Your ad failed to state (and to ask seems fair)
whether this opening is . . . tenure track?"

Now we both know it was a one-way tram.
Seven valiant souls inhabit the ozone,
and I'm alive to share your bitter dram.

Had they picked me, I would have gladly gone.
Instead, they chose and sacrificed a lamb,
and stuck me with this lump of frozen stone.

For here the satyr's mockery turns to ice.
The barb, transformed into an albatross,
burdens the archer and exacts its price.

'Tis cheap to moralize upon great loss.
Enough of words is wise, take my advice,
or they will let you stew in your own sauce.

But when I listen to the stream of cant
that issues from a simperer and a panderer,
I can't contain my wrath. I won't, I shan't!

Sauce for the goose is gravy for the gander.
So I invoke the Golden Rule of Kant,
in case I seem to stray or to meander.

When Theodosius or Bonapart
wished to exalt and to reform the Law,
they did not cast a lawyer in the part,

dress him in wings and build a nest of straw,
bundle him in and bid him, "Fly! Depart!"
and dare the devil beat him to the draw,

that Rome or France might crane her neck and gasp
to see the Law flying briefly like an eagle,
till gravity should reassert its grasp

and dash him down a pile of feathers legal;
nor did they inscribe their Codebook's golden hasp
with platitudes purloined from Erich Segal! *

   But we are governed by a different coterie.
By other arts you etch your works in granite:
your monument to Learning is the Lottery!

   Just warn us of your next "trip" when you plan it.
For, ostracized mid shards of astronautery,
we found ourselves upon the Seventh Planet.

   At least I felt at home on that odd ball
of bluegreen gas, where someone twice my age
is one, and dawn is all of youth, and fall

rings down the curtain and blacks out the stage
so that I've still not had my glimpse of *Sol*,
and methane is the medium and massage.

Voyager, not *Challenger*, transported us.
Yet you could not have asked for finer crew.
No fluke, no flaw, no negligence aborted us.

The lesson we transmit rings just as true
as if a high-school teacher had escorted us —
or even just a planetary Jew:

   "*Let Humankind be exalted as the end
of human striving, not to be degraded
to a lowly means to lofty dividend;*

---

* "Love means never having to say you're sorry!"
                                       — "*Love Story*"

let fluttering dreams be not in chains paraded
through star-studded streets to their dead end
as captive symbols of a goal evaded;

the tranquil gaze of intellect be not wrenched
by rhetoric of reaction pro and contra,
of leaders irredeemably entrenched,

nor by FX, flash-blinded in the antra
of imaging, nor thirst for knowledge quenched
by cultural sodapop and mystic mantra.

Permit no Freedom's hunger to be sated
on Liberty's accoutrement and trapping,
while Freedom lies denuded and abated;

take not for free-flying speech the feeble flapping
of conforming lips, albeit Nielsen-rated,
nor for plebiscite the pollster's random mapping.

Construe no constitution of a single
charter, erect no platform with one nail,
franchise no free election on a jingle,

make not a history out of one tall tale.
In short, don't put to sea upon a shingle,
or hoist a flag for use as a mainsail.

    And if you send a woman into space
(or two!), make sure you bring her back alive;
or else be quick and ready to replace

her as a mother and a loving wife,
instead of speechifying and showing your face
among the bereaved. Same goes for the other five!"

    Dante and I stood back to back, like Janus,
each scouring for a bridge his hemisphere,
that rare Convergence* in the diaphanous

* See note next page.

like steppingstones across an empty mere,
directing us away, far from Uranus.
    There's more to come, although the buck stops here!

> *Note: Convergence: a rare planetary alignment of Mercury, Venus, Earth, Mars, Jupiter, Saturn, the sun and the moon occurred on May 5, 2000, when according to the plan of Dante in Disneyland I encounter Dante in the "Magic Kingdom". That year, I would have reached the same age as Dante was when he died and (so I had premised) reappeared among the living.*

NON EXPLICIT PAUSA EST

The Mocking Bird (May 4, 2000)

After writing this sonnet, I realized that twenty-one years previously to the day, I was awakened at two in the morning by the lament of a mocking-bird in the family garden. It was the first time I had ever heard a mocking bird in nocturnal concert. His song was heartbreakingly beautiful. It was the morning of the funeral for my beloved Uncle Bronek—the great violinist, Bronislaw Gimpel, OHS.

The pittosporum mimes an exotic bloom
and fills my waking dreams with a heavy scent
and the scent that permeates my unshuttered room
is mingled with a strange and sad lament.

It is the sobbing of the mocking bird —
that silly creature who the whole day long
tattles and trills his tales of the absurd.
Now, none can miss the meaning of his song.

Little bird, what brings you to my garden weeping?
Was it you that, dreaming, I heard knocking, knocking?
To unlock the secrets I have long been keeping
and spill them to the stars, distant and mocking?

Then by your song I stand fully confessed.
Are you come for me? Then fly me to your nest!

To a Literary Agent (Nov. 21-22, 2001)

The Irish never persecuted Jews —
till now, that is, until the Celtic Muse,

turning up her pretty nose at kindred blood,
sought greener grass in Jewish neighbourhood.

Dipping her pen into the Holocaust,
she mulled o'er history's due and weighed the cost,

the mood, the market, and the current trends,
set pen to paper, and alerted Jewish friends.

O Joyce, *Oy vey!* O Beckett, and O'Casey!
Not every Jew dissolves in moist ecstasy

to see a Goy swap grief for guilt vicarious.
Repent! Repair! Redress! But poetry? Spare ye us!

Into what do tearful rhapsodes think they'll dupe us
by caroling *homo homini lupus*?

The Holocaust is not Cain killing Abel
in a sort of maudlin, penitential fable;

It is the war against the People of God,
Israel, among the Nations, *Am Echad*!

What is this stranger doing in our war chariot
as if to absolve us of Judas Iscariot?

Why is this witness testifying in court?
His testimony's just a book report!

In making poems from hard documentation,
can poets resist the inevitable temptation

to open doors, with their creative vision,
to questions and historical revision?

Let it be written, "This is what we did to them
with clinically executed stratagem!"

that truth be ne'er perverted against truth
and justice might hang on to its last tooth.

Let it be writ, "My fathers never spoke
of the war; and I was too afraid to poke

those ashes lest a hidden tongue of flame
shoot up and I be burnt alive with shame.

My fathers' are the questionable genes
I've passed on to my kids, now in their teens.

What should I tell, what teach, what method use
to assure they'll never don their fathers' shoes?"

Your poet is dancing at a stranger's wedding.
Has he nothing in a more congenial setting?

You say he's all agog to tour the U.S.
and hawk his books; but what will be his *shmuess*?

Should I not ask what is his Muse's agenda
before I book a six-month tour and send her?

Will he read, and in one sanctimonious breath
commend Jerusalem to a divided death?

Will he make a plea for a Palestinian state
and the right of Arabs to 'repatriate'?

Bid us share sovereignty with those who trample
our right to, and relics of, the Holy Temple?

Turn the other cheek to a bloody valentine
and hug to our breast the knife of Palestine?

Will he plead these things in the name of Jesus Crossed?
Or worse, in the name of Jesus Holocaust?

What need have we of Goyish poets' tears
to water graves wet with two thousand years?

Whether your poet-client is Celt or Jew,
I'd like those questions answered. Wouldn't you?

Perhaps one ought to know a little more
before one publishes poems on the Shoah!

The poems themselves aren't bad; indeed, quite good —
nice tourists in a foreign neighborhood —

a precinct even Jews approach with dread
and poets, till now, have wisely feared to tread.

God bless the Irish and your Irish bard!
Their heart is great, their lot, exceeding hard!

I love their women, whiskey, wit, and terriers,
above all, their poets! Let them respect some barriers!

God grant them health, prosperity and peace,
and everywhere on earth, may evil cease!

Basket Case (2002) To Herb Brin, after he unceremoniously hung up on me to watch the Lakers.

Brin (1915-2003) was the fearless and inimitable founding editor/publisher of Heritage, *for nearly five decades the landmark weekly newspaper of LA's Jewish Community. I made his acquaintance after he wrote a glowing review of* Twilight with Halfmoon Rising. *It was a great honor to be able to call him a friend.*

Hey what's so great about pro basketball?
Okay, so you can't be a total klutz.
But where's the challenge if you're seven-foot tall?
Besides, the squeaking really drives me nuts!

It's not a sport that takes a lot of guts.
And forget good manners! They're not required at all.
For example, see how often one guy cuts
the other off just when he's throwing the ball!

I still can't figure out how they keep score —
unless you're supposed to count the points those jocks
are scoring *off*, as well as *on*, the court!

If I could change the rules, I'd wax the floor
and send the old pros out there in their socks
and cut the rookies off at five-foot short!

At the Barber Shop (Aug. 22, 2006)

In the barber's chair
I think of a Vermeer
as visions of myself
unfold ad infinitum
reflected in the mirror

before me and behind
blank reflecting blank –
except, in endless procession
curling into obscurity
my hapless image
anxiously revolving
diminishing, receding
so that – but for its fading –
my image would remain
a captive of the barber shop
long after I have paid and gone.
As it is, I wonder
whether my image dying
endures somewhere between two worlds –
a dense and concentrated mass
a dimness all my own, pure and intense –
a single photon, even –
that, waterlike, preserves my aspect
long after all the light's been
wrung out of it
yet dings a bell
at opposite ends of the universe.
And when, still in the barber's chair
it suddenly occurs to me
that long have I – and not my image –
rebounded between two surfaces –
not mirrors – and with time, I muse
have neither faded nor receded nor diminished
but, on the contrary
grown brighter, sharper, closer –
the barber interrupts
holding up a mirror to my face
so that I may clinically inspect
the back of my unsuspecting neck.

Pseudo-Philodemi Poenitentia (around 2009)
Translated from the Greek of an unpublished papyrus.

O god of mystery, concealed by darkness, rememberest thou me?
Constant companion of my distant schooldays,
did we not wrestle often over books and verse
and rules of calculus and rhetoric and metre?
    Yea, thou who hoardest and dispensest knowledge,
thou who guardest the granaries of life and learning,
know that what thou suffered me to win from thee I long laid up
                                                         in store.
Yet, life being short, that which is remembered is soon forgotten.
I have rowed my years, and, as the poet (who, then?) sings
"What my net has caught I have sold to you."
And for good price! For thou hast left me reason, precious beyond
                                                                jewels!
Hear now my palinode and accept my repentance as an offering.
    Slave, go tell the Master: I am old and have missed the mark.
For though in life I pursued the way of truth and peace,
I am persuaded at the end that I have gone astray.
And you, O Memory, elusive god, now mock me wracked by time,
as, it is said, you mocked my master's master,
when in his feeble years he sensed the flight of reason from his
                                                                     breast
and deeming life without philosophy more burdensome than death,
                                                                     chose that.
    A paradox this unequivocalest end of ends
that shamelessly swallows up a life unto itself!
Memory, being the first to go, paves the way for self-control,
autonomy, objective thought, and continence,
the faculties, the teeth, like scattering sheep,
and after them, like sheepdogs in a frenzy,
the legs, as gravity and chaos overcome cohesive force.
Yet by your grace and boundless generosity,
reason's chamber still leased to me remains: I think,
though indolent and scatterbrained I waste my days,
my only exercise the endless chasing after names and dates.
Whom did I encounter at such or such a time?

And whether this or that he said, or was it someone else?
Who gave it me, that memorable wine? Where is that book?
What name did I confer on her — pet name — who taught me
amatory arts long put aside, alas, neglected and unused?
And where are the stars in which, by night, I took such
                                          limitless delight?

    Will you forgive, O God, my long neglect of you,
the casting from my mind the poignant recollection
of dear ones gone whom doctrine demurred to mourn?
Or do you but tap me triumphant on the shoulder,
as if to say, "Pardon, sir, but will you kindly cast your eye
in my direction? Teach me now, what do you see?"
    I see that you, O Memory, are One! I see Parmenides
in everlasting dance with free-falling Epikouros!
I see myself chastised among the blest
for I have sacrificed to you the bullocks of my days,
though I knew it not! And so I am rewarded!
    The small boy thinks he will hate young girls forever,
the lovesick youth that he will never recover
from the love he's lost. In the flower of my manhood
I looked too much forward to new horizons, vistas
to regret plowed fields behind that I loved best.
Now it is but memories I mourn. So much of life
is thoughtlessness. Without a key to unlock the vaults
of names and faces, tender words, the smiling gifts and gestures,
myself, too, I seem to have forgotten.
Who have I been? What were my works and days?
My deeds, good and bad, what were they, that I might account?
What? Shall I to the fire consign my tracts? The very flames
report to you my heresies, relay my errors.
Shall I sweep the continents for those I falsely taught?
Unteach my graduates, set them at this late date aright?
Have I been loved? Am I remembered? Was I of friendship worthy?
What am I now that so much of life has fled my grasp?
    One God I from my father learned, from my mother, many;
and so I followed him who taught no gods at all.
His Doctrine I recall—that is the irony—recall to disavow.
For what is this world if all that is be not recorded?

The whole knows itself as one or could not function.
That knowledge-of-self sustained through time is memory.
Hence Memory is unity, is all, suppressed all banishes like ostraka.
I have offended the All-knowing, the Unforgetting.
Yet naked, broken and abashed I stand recalled before you!
Thus have you, All-Forgiving, shorn the sheep of falsehood,
Thus have you loosed the blindfold from my eyes,
Thus have you cut the moorings of my past.
Now let us launch a black ship into the bright sea . . . *

      * Homer, *Iliad*, I, 141.

Chinese Interlude

1. Correspondence (around 2009)

An auspicious hour to sit here with a glass of wine
revisiting your letter and your poems
by dwindling candlelight
my answer wanting only brush and homemade ink.

Few behold from here the dipping of the moon
into the jewelry of a distant lake
or sense the chill of fragrance blowing upon the inquiring cheek;
few descry the ruin of princely gardens or meditate thereon.
Few indeed can understand this tongue. Our valuables are safe:
no need to lock them up!

Have you noticed how it is with poets?
They seem always to sing "the moon" –
not half a moon, not peel or paring of the moon,
not shades or inklings of the moon.
Our poets are like madmen —
bowled over when the moon is full,
not to be approached save through their verse!

Have you noticed, too, how the candles have gone out
with a shiver of unbraided smoke?
My answer to you wants but a brush.

2. Tonight the Moon (date unknown)

Tonight the moon
poses high above my head.
impudence to crane my neck
while she divests herself
of her white robes!
Half-hid among the leaves and branches
I observe her naked as she bathes.

3. Those Were Not Petals (2014)
After "The Flowering Tree" by Taiwanese poetess, Xi Murong

How to let you meet me
At the moment of my greatest beauty?
For this I stood before the Buddha for five hundred years.
Let us meet here in this earthly life!

So I became a tree by the roadside
where you pass by every day.
Under the sun I opened carefully my every blossom
each bloom my longing from my former life.

Next time when you approach, please pay attention!
Those trembling leaves were the passion of my waiting;
and when you thoughtless passed me by

the flowers that fell in your footsteps —
ah, friend, those were not petals!
They were the fragments of my withered heart!

4. Tonight, You Are the Moon (2014)

I do not know the author of these lovely verses. They are in the style of Xi Murong. They were given to me in translation by a most beautiful woman. I asked her, did she compose them? She would not tell me.

How to let you know?
I would walk around this world to find you.
Yet not one flower can I allow to speak for me;
not to a single leaf can I entrust my longing.
Tonight, outside my window, you are the moon.
If you listen with your heart,
you will hear as in a dream
a voice calling your name.
But do not tell anyone.
Let it be our secret!

5. There are no Secrets (2014)

Truly outside your window
I am like the waiting moon
shining its quiet light
upon your face and in your heart.
All the flowers speak of this.
All the leaves are trembling with this.
Who calls my name in dreams but you?
Who is there who does not know but you?
Can you not hear the moon?
There are no secrets.
I too have walked around the world.
I am tired. I have found no rest but you.

6. Moon Festival (2014)

On this night of courtship and rebellion
Let us assemble the sixteen pieces
and by the light of the full moon
unwrap the secret of immortal love!
To overthrow darkness and darkness
in one brave, exquisite bite!

7. Ideogram

Wild geese do not intend to cast a reflection
and water has no mind to retain it. *
Yet in my mind
I see the geese
the clear water
and the reflection
also the poem
and the one who wrote it
perhaps with a quill
from one of those same geese
writing on the water
that heeds the reflection.
Not one of those things
could exist without the other.
It is for this they were created.
The intent, the mind, the image, the poem.
How vast, this one character —
Wild geese flying over water!

* Old Zen saying

8. Asian Lilies

Oriental bloom
exhaling perfume!
Thy scent now through tears of dew!

A Green Haze (March 31, 2013)

This morning, I saw apple trees
wrapped in a green haze.
What is this haze of green?
It is the glow of spring
just dropping by to visit with my apples.
I too feel a greeny glow.
What is this glow of green?

It is the glow of spring
paying her respects to an aging man.
Just nodding, just passing by . . .

Fire Break (2013)

I love those tractor paths etched in that hill
that yearn and burn to reach the rounded crest
and lose their grip sometimes and grab the slope
as if by sheer force of some immanent will,

and claw back up again to round a bend
and bulldoze blindly on, losing neither hope
nor ingenuity, and knowing no rest,
yet all to no purpose, and, it seems, no end.

Those clean sharp trails cut through the gilded stubble
that lead to some imaginary yonder
give me pause to meditate, and wonder

Why would someone go to all that trouble
to plow such paths that stray whither they will —
and I with no choice but to climb that hill!

Neanderthal (April 16, 2013)

Recent studies suggest
that Homo sapiens sapiens
did not annihilate Neanderthal neanderthal
but interbred with him.
Which would explain
why two species coexist
in what we call a man.
Perhaps we should give thanks
that this, too, we have survived?

Adolescence (May, 2013) Vincenzo Cardarelli (1887-1959)

On you, virgin adolescent,
rests a kind of sacred shadow.
Nothing is more mysterious
adorable and proper
than your flesh unclothed.
But you recluse yourself in your neat *complet*
and live aloof
with your gracefulness
where you wonder who is to have you.
Dear me, not I! If I see you pass
at such royal remove
your hair let down,
all your body a spear,
I am carried off by dizziness.
You are the creature smooth and impervious
upon whom weighs in its breath
the dark rejoicing of the flesh that barely
supports its own fullness.
In the blood that diffuses
flame upon your face
the cosmos emits its laughter.
Like the black eye of a swallow,
your pupil is consumed
by the sun that burns there.
Shuttered is your mouth.
Your white hands know not
the abasement of sweaty contact.
And I think how your body,
problematic and vague,
makes love despair
in the heart of man.
Yet someone *will* deflower you,
artesian spring.
Someone who will not know,
a sponge fisher,
will have this exquisite pearl.

It will be his good grace and fortune
to not look for you,
to not know who you are,
to not enjoy you
with the subtle sensuality
that offends the jealous God.
Oh yes, the animal will be
thickheaded enough
not to die before he touches you.
So it always goes.
You too have no idea who you are.
You will let yourself be taken —
if only to see how the game is played,
if only to laugh a bit together.
As a flame loses itself in the light,
at the first peep of reality
your promised revelations
dissolve into nothing.
Unconsummated must pass
such ecstasy!
You will give yourself, you will lose yourself
to the caprice that never guesses right,
to the first whom you shall fancy.
Time favors the joke
that plays along,
not desire circumspect and lingering.
Thus it is nonage
makes the world spin round
and the wise man is only a little boy
who grieves that he is grown.

That Coltish Look (November 13, 2013)

You're into surfaces more than you should be.
Admit it, man, you're something of a rogue!
You've set your sights on a blonde who really could be
one of those coltish fillies draped in *Vogue*.

Box seats at the opera, boxes of chocolates, you
old dog! Dinner and dance, champagne and roses . . .
You can afford to splurge, so long your stock lets you —
or until a nebbish she's been seeing proposes.

She at first accepts, then missing all the attention,
phones you, vacillates, changes her mind.
You win the prize; the jock, the honorable mention.
The honeymoon cruise is on the Golden Hind.

Years pass. You view the marriage with remorse,
and think, "My God! She *does* look like a horse!"

The True Story of the Lobster and the Octopus (December, 2013, revised November 22, 2020)

(*In its natural habitat, the octopus has a dietary predilection for lobster.*)

    Do animals not know true love? I mean
love free from prejudice, dictates of gene,

ulterior motive — *arrière pensée*,
food chains broken for interspecies play —

the fox gamboling with a fluffy troupe
of chippering tenants of the chicken coop?

Does not the billygoat calm horses' nerves?
Don't dogs make friends in elephant preserves?

Was a drowning youth not saved by a dolphin's fins?
Did a she-wolf not give suck to the Roman Twins?

Who can forget Koko, the gorilla smitten
with love for All Ball — tiny, fearless kitten?

I kept an ancient tortoise once, a jay
harassed her till a crow chased him away.

I've witnessed the self-immolation of an ant
in deference to some altruistic covenant,

that her companion might survive a felony
to drag a carcass to her hungry colony.

Once, musing mournfully at the Aquarium,
"Mutabilis est femina et varium,"

I paused before a picture-window tank
in which an eccentric octopus broke rank

with its own species and affiliation
to indulge an arthropodal fascination —

as if to mend a broken heart's left ventricle
with lobster's claw and octopus's tentacle.

I remember watching them in tender awe
lying each in the other's tentacle and claw.

The story told in answer to my query,
by a mouse who witnessed it and turned canary,

is that the octopus and the crustacean,
impatient of their long-distance flirtation

through double glass and several feet of space,
the former, with the genius of his race,

contrived to switch between contiguous tanks,
by undulating, quite unnoticed (thanks

to the nonfeasance of the nightwatch guards
oblivious in a guilty game of cards),

and slithering and suctioning his way,
Leander to Hero Nephropidae.

Headlines in the news! "Don't Be Alarmed!
Escapee Called Not Dangerous, Though Armed."

The guards were sacked, as might have been expected,
but by and by, the truant was detected

when a student intern noticed a new rock
in the lobster tank, and gave the glass a knock.

The rock snapped to and jetted to make cozy
with his new consort, he all flushed and rosy.

In fact, the octopus evinced such solace,
the staff nicknamed the couple Ed and Wallis.

(A lobster's sentiments are hard to plot
until they're dropped into a boiling pot.)

Alas, the lifespan Edward's species hath
is brief, the lobster's, long: you do the math.

Vita brevis est, sed amor brevior.
Between true love and mismatched, which is heavier?

   I fantasize those two had met before —
perhaps along some cold Atlantic shore,

perhaps within some warm Pacific reef,
and that their love was hindered by deep grief

among oystered pearls and sea-sequestered coral
occasioned by some crisis or some quarrel.

   Is there a Force that governs whom we love,
that matches lamb with lion, hawk with dove,

where each possesses something the other lacks
besides the obvious attributes of sex?

Or must a soul divide and take refuge
in misfit species through some subterfuge

that intervenes to spoil too easy happiness
lest joy disintegrate in soapy sappiness?

Why should two hearts conjoined by thunderclap
be split by trawler's net or lobster trap?

And why, if virtuous love must be cut short
is love called sinful when indulged for sport?

   I notice, too, that in the world of plants
there's something like companionship — romance

'twixt diverse species known to be compatible
when juxtaposed — both edible and inedible.

Judicious grafting, too, has given rise
to exotic fruits and sweet varieties.

   Yet Jewish Law forbids mixing and matching
in reference to grafting, sowing and batching;

and also, much to my chagrin, to dating,
lest selfless loving lead to procreating.

For God has taken us for His very own
and desires not to share us out on loan;

so gave us laws of breeding and of sowing
that no excuse be found in our not knowing,

or in our Patriarchs' being forced to choose
our Matriarchs from folks who were not Jews.

   Now neither 'pus nor lobster is a Jew;
and Jewish though I am, those blissful two

remain for me a symbol of the mystery
of interspecies love. Call this a history,

a tale of ill-starred love, call it a sob story —
a tale of octopusery and lobstery,

of Montagues and Capulets, once leading
to corruption of the flesh through interbreeding,

to violence, the shedding of much blood,
and the earth's being purged by universal flood.

   Yet what I see in it is something pure —
a love completely selfless, chaste, demure —

for all Creation — *and* for the Creator —
the God Who is One, the Great Multiplicator

Who wants each one of this diverse, vast drove
to restore His Oneness through our selfless love.

   So much of seeing has roots in the unseen:
Maia desnuda, mute behind her screen,

the iceberg's tip, the pine tree's spreading canopy,
the neuron's thought, imagination's panoply,

the origin of love, the magic potion
that lights a fire beneath the deep, dark ocean.

Francesca & Paolo: Dante's *Inferno: Canto 5* (March, 2014)

    So I descended from the outer ring
to the next one down, which lesser space entails
but greater pain, and more grief with its sting.

There Minos horribly stands and snarls and yells.
Examining the guilt of each entrant,
he judges and dispatches by his tail's

dictate. That is to say, the miscreant
approaches him and all its sins confesses;
and sin's great connoisseur, that recreant,

reflects where it belongs in hell's recesses.
With his tail, he winds himself as many coils
around as steps to where its new address is.

Before him a great crowd forever roils.
Each in his turn draws near him for the judging;
they speak, they hear, and downward each recoils.

"O you who venture into this dread lodging,"
said Minos when he noticed me, nonplussed,
as he broke off from his officious drudging,

"Take heed where you are going and whom you trust!
Let not the wideness of the gate mislearn ye!"
    To him replied my captain, "Why d'you bluster?

Do not attempt to impede his fateful journey:
So is it willed where will and might are one
and what is willed is done. More don't concern ye."

    And now begins a mournful, keening tone
to penetrate my ears. Now was I come
to where much grieving pierced me to the bone.

I came to a place where light is mute and gloam,
that roars like oceans mustered by tempest
when warred by opposing winds and whipt to foam.

The hurricanes of hell that know no rest
o'erwhelm the spirits with their turbulence
and tumbling, turning, battering, them molest.

When they approach the crumbling battlements,
there the shrieks, the groans and the grim gnashing!
There they blaspheme the Name, the impenitents!

I understood that to such style of thrashing
are damned the spirits tainted with ill fame
who, spurning reason, after lust went dashing.

   Then, as the starling's wings in winter claim
the skies, lift them in legions broad and full,
so the wind those sorry souls lifts quite the same;

so here, so there, so up and down, no lull.
No hope, no comfort ever stands them nigh
of lesser pain, of gentler push and pull.

And like the cranes that sing their lays and fly
configuring in the air a drawn-out row,
I saw come toward me with a woeful sigh

some shadows swept by the aforesaid tow.
Whereupon, I queried, "Maestro, who are those
the black wind buffets and chastises so?"

   "The foremost of the pair of whom you chose
to ask," replied the latter, "know that she
was imperatrix of much land and chose,

so tainted with the vice of luxury,
that in her reign was lechery made law
to camouflage her own ignominy.

That was Semíramis, whom you just saw,
who both succeeded Ninus and him wed.
She held the lands now neath the Sultan's paw.

The other, self-immolate on the bed
in which Sychaeus' dust still warm, she shamed.
Just now, spoiled Cleopatra by us sped.

Now Helen see, whose folly is justly blamed
for so much blood. Look! There's the great Peleides,
whose lust chaste Polyxena falsely tamed.

Look! Paris! Tristan!" A thousand knights' and ladies'
shades and more he showed, and knew by fame
how love of luxury sent them all to Hades.

    When my good doctor finished, name by name,
the list of ancient maids and cavaliers,
compassion touched me and almost overcame.

"I'd so love, Poet," I ventured through my tears,
to speak with them, who joined together fly
more lightly in the wind, so it appears."

    And he to me: "Wait till they're closer by;
and then implore them gently to abide,
by the love that leads them, and they will comply."

    As soon the wind had brought them near our side,
I moved my voice: "O troubled spirits, please
come speak with us, if that be not denied."

As mourning doves called by their fledglings' pleas,
wings raised and stilled before the gentle nest,
borne thither by their will, come through the breeze,

so, leaving Dido's group at my behest,
made they their way to us through the air malign,
so heartfelt was the friendship I professed.

"O living soul, so gracious and benign,
who sightseeing go through purple air and black,
we two, whose wounds the world incarnadine,

if we did not the Lord's good graces lack,
for you and for your peace to Him we'd pray,
since you take pity on our mourning black.

Whatever pleases you to hear or say,
we will be glad to hear and say to you
as long the wind stays calm here out the way.

   "The land and town where I was born and grew
sits on the coast where the Po River flows
to sea in peace with tributaries two.

Love, who's swift to teach pure hearts its throes
took hold this swain of that of which I'm shorn —
my comely form — and how 'twas shorn still shows.

Love, who leaves no one who is loved forlorn,
possessed me of a love for him so great
that as you see, we're still together borne.

Love guided us as one to a single fate.
Cain waits for him by whom our lives were rent."
   Such were the things they ventured to relate.

When I had grasped those wounded souls' lament,
I lowered my eyes and kept them long *à bas*,
till the poet said, "On what are you intent?"

When I replied at last, I said, "Alas!
How many dreams, what powerful desire
have led those two to such a dreadful pass!"

Then turning to them both, I made to inquire,
and spoke: "Francesca, all your agonies
fill me with sorrow, and penitence inspire;

but, at the time of your first dulcet sighs,
say how and in what guise did love consent
to acquaint you with such dubious enterprise?"

And she to me: "No greater punishment
than to recall one's former happiness
in mis'ry! This knows well your good docent!

But if you crave to know how did progress
our love from its first tender root, I'll be
as one who weeps and talks nevertheless.

One day we sat reading alternately,
one to the other, how Lancelot loved the queen.
We were alone, from all suspicion free;

and sitting side by side, the book between,
our reading turned our eyes, reddened our face.
But only at one point did we give in.

'Twas when we read how her sweet smile of grace
was kissed by such renowned and ardent lover:
this one, whom time shall ne'er from me displace,

kissed me right on the mouth, trembling all over.
Gallant was the bard, his book, our guide.
We set the book aside and closed the cover."

While the one spirit said this, the other cried,
and wept so piteously such waterfalls,
I felt myself fade out as if I died,

and fell to earth as a dead body falls!

Driving to Vegas (April 14, 2014)

Death Valley alive
with Joshua trees
pleading, gesticulating.

A Passing Thought (November 3, 2014)

I just remembered
there used to be a flower
called forget-me-not.

To the Abstainers (March 4, 2015)

On March 3, 2015, Binyomin Netanyahu, the Prime Minister of Israel, addressed a Joint Meeting of the United States Congress to plead against the adoption of a demonstrably ineffectual Joint Comprehensive Plan of Action (Iran Nuclear Deal) with an extremist regime that had repeatedly threatened to destroy the Jewish State. Eight Senators and fifty Representatives (listed below) boycotted Netanyahu's address. Bless God! the remaining circa 477 Legislators welcomed the Prime Minister with cheers and a standing ovation that went on for more than 4 minutes. The Prime Minister's Address was received with no less enthusiasm. Three years and two months later, the US announced its withdrawal from the Iran Nuclear Deal.

Affecting umbrage at the purported slight
to the President
to the "Sanctity of the House"
at the "assault on diplomacy,"
anachronists, invoking lèse majesté,
you absented yourselves
indignant that a Jewish leader should presume
to accept an invitation by the Speaker of the House —
my House —
to voice misgivings
(his, mine and many of your own Constituents')
about peace-partnering with an enemy
proven treacherous
self-declared unscrupulous
untrustworthy and intransigent
inveterate swindlers of the bazaar
faced by amateurs and upstarts

naifs and sophomores —
"chickenshits" (to use a term of late
inducted into the State
Department Lexicon)
who hold the fate of millions in their hands.
It bothers you that Israel
whose interest in the matter
is a thousand times greater than yours,
whose existence is the essence of these talks,
unspoken and undistilled,
should speak its mind?
   What gives those callow valedictorians
presumptuous meddlers of "C" Street
gamesters, wreckers of the peace
the audacity to barter with the fate of a nation not their own,
and you to stifle its voice
and turn your backs on its concerns?
   Where do you find the face to crawl out of your hole
after the bombshell
to defend your obtuse inhumanity
and criticize, distort and dismiss the very words
you peevishly refused to hear?
You, the Honorable Abstainers,
Senators and Representatives, big heroes
you preening sanctimonious smug fool champions
of propriety and protocol
you craven hypocrites,
posers and brownnosers
brownshirts, too, perhaps among you,
xenophobes and Jewhaters:
What do you represent?
What school did you go to?
Who taught you?
Who raised you?
Who elected you?
What church or synagogue do you attend?
You bring dishonor to them all.
Slink back into your hole,
Honorable Abstainers!

SENATE - 8 members

Sen. Al Franken (Minn.)
Sen. Martin Heinrich (N.M.)
Sen. Tim Kaine (Va.)
Sen. Patrick Leahy (Vt.)
Sen. Bernie Sanders (I-Vt.)
Sen. Brian Schatz (Hawaii)
Sen. Elizabeth Warren (Mass.)
Sen. Sheldon Whitehouse (R.I.)

[Sen. Diane Feinstein (California)]. Sen. Feinstein did not abstain, but earned an honorary place among the Abstainers for comments she made to Dana Bash on CNN's "State of the Union", March 1, 2015:

DB: *"When Netanyahu says he's coming to speak, he says he speaks for all Jews. Does he speak for you?"*

Sen. F: *"He doesn't speak for me on this. He doesn't at all speak for me on this."*

DB: *"Does it bother you when he says he speaks for all Jews?"*

Sen. F.: *"Yah, I think it's a rather arrogant statement . . . I think arrogance does not befit Israel, candidly."*

Sen. Feinstein said these things three days before Purim, the Jewish Festival commemorating the salvation of the Jewish People from total annihilation by Haman, the Biblical forerunner of the present Iranian regime. She said it at the very moment the Jews of the Bible were fasting for their (and our) survival. Sen. Feinstein has made good political capital from her Jewish name, but, her halachic Jewishness has been questioned. Surely, the answer to that question came from her own mouth.

HOUSE - 50 members

Rep. Karen Bass (Calif.)
Rep. Earl Blumenauer (Ore.)
Rep. Corrine Brown (Fla.)
Rep. G.K. Butterfield (N.C.)
Rep. Lois Capps (Calif.)
Rep. Andre Carson (Ind.)
Rep. Joaquin Castro (Texas)
Rep. Katherine Clark (Mass.)
Rep. William Lacy Clay (Mo.)
Rep. James Clyburn (S.C.)
Rep. Emanuel Cleaver (Mo.)
Rep. Steve Cohen (Tenn.)
Rep. Bonnie Watson Coleman (N.J.)

Rep. John Conyers (Mich.)
Rep. Elijah Cummings (Md.)
Rep. Danny Davis (Ill.)
Rep. Peter DeFazio (Ore.)
Rep. Diana DeGette (Colo.)
Rep. Lloyd Doggett (Texas)
Rep. Rosa DeLauro (Conn.)
Rep. Donna Edwards (Md.)
Rep. Chaka Fattah (Pa.)
Rep. Keith Ellison (Minn.)
Rep. Marcia Fudge (Ohio)
Rep. Raúl Grijalva (Ariz.)
Rep. Luis Gutiérrez (Ill.)
Del. Eleanor Holmes Norton (D.C.)
Rep. Eddie Bernice Johnson (Texas)
Rep. Marcy Kaptur (Ohio)
Rep. Rick Larsen (Wash.)
Rep. Barbara Lee (Calif.)
Rep. John Lewis (Ga.)
Rep. Dave Loebsack (Iowa)
Rep. Zoe Lofgren (Calif.)
Rep. Betty McCollum (Minn.)
Rep. Jim McDermott (Wash.)
Rep. Jim McGovern (Mass.)
Rep. Jerry McNerney (Calif.)
Rep. Gregory Meeks (N.Y.)
Rep. Gwen Moore (Wis.)
Rep. "Beto" O'Rourke (Texas) ("the Skateboard Candidate")
Rep. Donald Payne (N.J.)
Rep. Chellie Pingree (Maine)
Rep. David Price (N.C.)
Rep. Cedric Richmond (La.)
Rep. Jan Schakowsky (Ill.)
Rep. Adam Smith (Wash.)
Rep. Bennie Thompson (Miss.)
Rep. Mike Thompson (Calif.)
Rep. John Yarmuth (Ky.)

For me, this "abstention" was the first undisguised manifestation of an anti-Semitic crick in the neck of US politics that has since become increasingly noticeable under the erratic leadership of Speaker Pelosi, and increasingly painful through the antics of the adventurist "Gang of Four."

A Sense of Loss (March 9, 2015)

A small bird lighted on a post.
It pleased me in a special way.
For one second I looked away.
When I looked back, the bird was lost

I opened my window in the morning light
My blue spruce was festooned with flowers.
I looked again after a few hours
and my blue spruce was blue as night.

The bird, I think, was real, the flowers, not.
The sense of loss that each hath brought
makes sense of my unformulated thought.

The Turtle's Complaint (May 12-27, 2015)

An old sea-turtle in a tortoise shell
pined for the seas in which he used to dwell.
A pond frog living as a desert toad
condoled with him over their scorched abode
but pinned this ending to his villanelle:
"Don't you complain – at least you have a shell!"

Zen Pond (June, 2004 / August 16, 2015)

Even as a child I used to peer
into a dark pond delighting
to observe the bronzen moon
at parlance with the fishes.
They were glints of something
slippery as a woman's logic
in the ambiguity of water.
She, however, has nixed the idea.
Now staring into a Zen pond
I watch my own thoughts
darting every which way
in the sweetsmelling void.

Breakfast News (August 5, 2015)

Rustling the pages of *The Times*
over my cereal, orange juice and coffee
I read that Professor Hawking –
warns us urgently
not to search for alien intelligence
lest we find some
and they consider us good protein.
    Another page reports:
"UFO Sightings On the Rise"
but doesn't specify
whether this be due
to a statistical increase
in the number of flying saucers,
or just more people looking up.
    In fact, the number of unemployed
according to another item
is also on the rise! Coincidence?
The Literary Section features a book review
about a scientist (advisor to the President)
who claims that we are just bacteria
with overgrown brains.
    The label on my kefir bottle
says that every serving contains
seven billion CFUs
of live and active cultures
all working to keep me healthy and regular.
That's about the same number
as the population here on earth . . .
    My box of muesli (just add milk)
displays a picture of ET.
His caption reads (get this!):
Breakfast is the most important meal of the Day!
    Here's my Letter to the Editor:
"Professor Hawking has an overblown
opinion of humanity.
We are not protein.
We are probiotics.
And just enough
to get one constipated alien
going again."

Bogeys (May 18, 2017)

Last night, at Tom's, as we were saying goodbye,
I happened to look up. A UFO
was hovering high above me in the sky —
a kind of disk or wheel inside an oval.

In the wheel, something like a bug's eye —
revolving, glowing an eerie grayish glow.
It began to move, drifting in total silence,
slowly heading north toward Frisco.

"Hey look!" I yelled to Tom, "Do you see *that?*"
Tom craned his neck and searched the sky. "See what?"
"Flying saucer," I replied. "No," he said, flat.

The incident left me with an odd feeling,
later, when a bogey buzzed me, wheeling,
as I lay in bed, just staring at the ceiling!

The Color of Sky Before Snow (Dec. 19, 2012; revised Dec. 4, 2015)

Recall the color of sky before it snowed —
the unsavory and impenetrable grey
that would dismay if it did not forebode
the pretense of pure white the sky will lay
upon our snowbedazzled eyes below,
like something pure, unsullied and intact;
as if it strove to conceal some ugly fact —
the septic truth behind the whitewashed cause;
the prismancy of crystals a soothing gauze
that, spread upon our retinae to refract
its light into a whitedrugged artifact
of optic ecstasy and afterglow,
though blindingly, though blandishingly bright,
adapts that truth to our frail and squeamish sight.

The Flowering Pear (Feb. 24/25, 2015)
To my dear son.

Today I planted a tree—a flowering pear —
my favorite flowering tree, a mere sapling,
its first green leaves just starting to appear.
And I, no longer green (not old!), still grappling
with old questions, now ask, "Will I be there
when this fine tree, sturdy and tall, assumes
its mantle and its crown of white-hot blooms?"

Was planting it an act of faith or kindness?
I'd hope to see the fruit of all my labors
(God save me from untimely death or blindness!)
but if I can't, I'd want to please my neighbors
and be remembered for my staunch onemindness
to follow the example of this tree
and flower with it to my maturity.

The Rocking Chair (Sept. 6-8, 2015)
To my darling daughter for her 21st Birthday

When you were five — you were just a piece of fluff —
you wanted a little rocking chair - your size.
That was enough.
So I built one from a kit
and you sat in it.
Never will I forget your eyes
solemn and alive with wonder and delight.
That was perhaps my greatest happiness!
Except maybe when my old mother
first held you in her arms, beaming.
    Actually, there *was* another.
You wanted a doll house to play with, dreaming.
I thought I'd build you one out of the box.
It took a while for me to realize
I'd have to buy you one ready-made.
It wasn't cheap: almost had to take out a loan!

But the way you clapped your hands, jumping up and down . . .
That was the happiest of all!
That was the crown!
It had two storeys, a roofed porch and colonnade —
which you promptly turned toward the wall!
It was the inside that mattered to the woman —
not the façade!
    Now that the woman is fully grown
it's not so easy to fulfil your wishes —
or even know exactly what they are.
A good husband will buy you a real house,
two sets of silverware and dishes, and a car,
and in your old, old age, your sons, a rocking chair
for you to sit in, knitting
woolens for your grand and great grandchildren.
    I can see you with your sweet smile, sitting,
rocking, remembering, murmuring *Tehillim*
listening to the needles clicking
and, like me, to the clock quietly ticking.

Fandango (Nov. 24 - 29, 2015)

Roused by fingerings of guitars
I draw the curtains, and looking out
I see a stand of poplars
extruded in the pale cold sun
like vibrant strings tuned taut and true.
Gold sparks shoot through a sky cold blue.
Soon those trees will all be bare,
transparent to music, light and air.
Already the ground is laid with yellow.
"Nothing new in this, young fellow,"
proclaims my wise old trickster friend.
"We've seen it all before, no end."
He cackles softly like castanets.
His cronies in flamenco black
twirl stately in the wailing wind
as the wind's cold fingers burn the frets.

The Voice in the Mirror (Dec. 25, 2015)

"I am not sure which of us is writing this page."
                                                    J.L. Borges, "Borges and I"

While shaving in the mirror, it occurred to me
that what with rising steam the world looked blurred to me
and trying to reconstruct a dream, still groggy
I slid to think of thought. My thought was foggy
for behind the foggy glass, a blurry image
locked eyes with me in a kind of staring scrimmage.
I was the first to speak, my voice still hoarse
from sleep — or was it his? But in the course
of speaking (he and I), I realized
the content wasn't mine, but plagiarized —
don't know from where — from him or me, I suppose.
It was a poem, the original in prose.
But when it was done, the two of us switched place
and I no longer recognized my face!

Some Thoughts on Superman (March 1-2, 2016)

Taken out of context, the cry is absurd.
Also sprach Zarathustra: "It's a bird!"
Or, more accurately, "*Schau! Ein Vogel!*"
"*Nein, ein Flugzeug!*" "*Nein, 'sist Übermensch!*"
   That's not exactly what Nietzsche had in mind.
The umlaut would have looked ridiculous
emblazoned on his chest over the U.
And U is better left for academe.
A black *Reichsadler* with a Swastika
might have worked if things had turned out different.
   Of course, the cry was not aimed at a sky
immemorable of birdsong or of flight
but at some aerial object unidentified.
Already then we ached for aliens
pinning our hopes on ET saviors
over machines and denizens of earth.
The *deus ex machina* of Euripides.
The Messianic or Mosaic dream

conveyed by comic books more clearly
and more effectively than by the Bible.
    As a child I too looked up for Superman.
Had Mama sew an "S" on my pajamas,
throw me a costume party for my birthday.
Sizing myself up in her bedroom mirror
I didn't notice that my mom had sewn
the "S" on in reverse — like "Ambulance"
in a rearview mirror. A mother's wisdom
is not always deliberately imparted.
    Eventually, I weaned from my obsession
and learned in time to think more critically.
Found out I didn't need to be a superman
to "leap tall buildings in a single bound."
A man-sized flea could jump ten storeys high
and even Dad, when driving me to school
could travel "faster than a speeding bullet" —
if "speeding" meant going over 35 —
and Dad had evidence to prove it did!
    I had no hopes of ever matching Dad,
no Kafka dream of morphing into flea.
So I moved on to literature. I burnt
a fortune in my comic books and felt
ashamed of all my childish fantasies.
I hid the home movie my father made —
that mortifying and motley grand parade
of cowboys, Indians, pirates, assorted beasts
and a kid in blue pajamas, cape, and "⅂"
emblazoned on his chest. I kept it mum
but somehow — don't know how — the word got out.
The wife got hold of it and never let go.
For twenty years of that Xanthippic yoke
whatever I did, she'd kvetch, "Whatever you do,
you always do ess-backwards!" Maybe so,
but all I knew to answer in retort
was, "With a U - umlaut, you'd never know!"
But I'm afraid she never got the joke

(it took me many years till I got hers).
   But in the end I think Nietzsche was right.
His "God is dead" was only *Gott mit uns*;
there's still an Umlaut over Übermensch!
The problem is that every man believes
that since he seems to be the very center
of everything he sees and hears and thinks,
the universe must share his point of view.
And if it doesn't, then all his wits are lost.
Else how could he blow up the world to S-
O-S?
      The universe is not a mirror.
What's backwards in it backwards must remain
until of its free will it turn around.
   You know? Sometimes I hear the question asked:
"Suppose you had your choice of super powers:
what power would you bestow on the human race?"
And I think, "To each, the power to see his face."

Ceci n'est pas (March 28-30, 2016)
After Holbein's "Deposition" in Basel's *Kunstmuseum*.

It is reported that when Dostoevsky visited the Kunstmuseum, he was so entranced by this painting that his wife had to drag him away lest it give him an epileptic fit. Dostoevsky recalls the moment in his novel, The Idiot, *in which Prince Myshkin, the protagonist, viewing the same painting, exclaims, "Why, a man's faith might be ruined by looking at that picture!" It is often said that this is because the realism is so brutal as to negate the resurrection. However, I don't believe that is what troubled Dostoevsky. There is another explanation.*

A man, no doubt an ordinary man,
is thrown, or throws himself, into the Rhine
whence he is fished and carried to the morgue.
There, he is stretched out naked on a plank,
apotheosed in paints as Christ Deposed,
the air already rank with putrefaction,
his limbs tinged blue, mouth open, eyes unclosed.
The masterpiece inspires a deathless novel.
Is irony in heaven, or just enigma?

Is meaning married to, or marred by matter?
If worthy, he emaciates the message;
if not, he fouls the message with the fraud.
The paradox almost provokes a seizure;
the novel draws it out to the last page.

Memory as a Convex Mirror (Dec. 15/22, 2014)
After a Self-Portrait by Parmigianino.

It must be said outright: Parmigianino left deliberate clues which others, starting with Vasari, have missed. The artist painted himself as if reflected, but the left hand, poised as if holding a mirror, is empty! The palette and brushes are similarly hidden from view! The painting is a physical representation of a mental skill cultivated from the early Renaissance onward. Leon Battista Alberti, born a century before Parmigianino, is said to have excelled at it, as noted by Burckhart.

The focus is neither the portrait nor the painter;
but the critics and at least one flummoxed poet
mistook the foreground's exquisite dovelike hand
and the inward smile of the cloistered prosopon
savant and pregnant with its unspoken word
for figured conceit of his prodigious art
as though the hand — *mind you, the left* — were holding —
but where are the *brushes* if not outside the frame
where they rightly are if the right be coyly working
a mere surface — which the painting isn't, being pure space?
The hand reflected as if *in speculo*
holds what is seen but by the inner eye
something that makes it overfull and empty,
weightless yet ponderous — a huge transparent bird.

The Gift (November–December, 2017). For Alex Forbes

". . . and for your birthday I have sculpted you,"
confided my friend over the telephone.
I thought "exculpated" was the word he used.
But no, it was a sculpture he was talking of, and "huge!"
He'd done it all from memory, and would be mailing it.
They UPSed it some days later, while I was in the shower.

They were supposed to telephone but *OOPS!* they didn't.
Supposed to give a window — you know, an ETA
so I'd be home? Well, home I was, but didn't hear the door
so they left. Taking the statue with them, of course.
Or whatever it was. They left a sticker, which I didn't see
till I gave up waiting, and went out to buy some cheese.
I saw the sticker when I shut the door — much good that did.
The check boxes were all unchecked, but the numbers tracked.
I'd have to pick it up in flatland, down the hill —
Mojave, by the spaceport, past Baja's Bar & Grill.
  I phoned OOPS what I thought of driving twenty miles
and back and could I expect my paycheck in the mail.
Besides, what if it didn't fit into my KIA?
(Great little auto, by the way, but no trunk space!)
  "It shount be a problem. It weighs 5 pounds," she said,
"and it'll be a week before they try again.
Suppose you're out. They'll ship it back. What then?"
  So I drove down to Tomorrowland. No rocket ships.
No Right Stuff. Just a scattering of warehouses
in a George Herriman sundown. A frantic hour
going round and round like a toy car on a table.
  I found the distribution hub a minute before closing.
But for the dismal porchlight, it was night and finster dark.
The lady took my sticker, retreated to the rear —
after instructing someone on her cell about the steaks.
She reappeared, dwarfed by a box she dandled in her palms
as if air and packing-peanuts were all there was inside.
  "How'm I gonna get this in my car?" I asked. Rhetorically.
  "Dint you axe how big it was? You shoudda drove your truck!"
  "What truck? I did," I said indignantly. "I axed!
Customer Service said it weighed five pounds!"
(Customer Service was plainly she. I knew the voice.)
  "Honey, that's what it says here on the manifest.
Excuse me, please, I gotta shut the lights. It's late.
Was closing when you showed. Been home in bed by now . . ."
  So I shlepped the box out to my wagon, which I got a fix on
when a vagrant locomotive spat out a gob of sickly light
rounding a railroad bend, because the sconce was off.
  "No way José," I muttered, "will this ever fit!"
I edged back in a snit to where I judged the building was,

pushed through the portal just as she was locking up.
   "Look here," I said. "It won't go in. Please have your van . . ."
   "Sir, come back tomorrow, and fill out a shipping form."
   "Say what? The sender paid for full delivery! Now why . . ."
   "Sir, you arguin' with the weather. Nite! We're closed!"
   "Could you loan me a box cutter?" I pleaded from the stoop."
   After a senseless minute pounding on the door
an empty wine bottle winked at me from the desert floor
in a sweep of headlights from her outbound SUV.
I picked it up, I kissed it, smashed it on the steps
and used a shard to slash the cardboard open. Also my finger.
"Nuts!" I said. "Some kind of cockeyed joke! This is insane!"
   Finally, I pulled the shredded flaps apart. The contents —
even more voluminous now they'd been unpacked —
revealed themselves a block of polyurethane —
a cosmic mass of quantum foam in full-blown Guth expansion —
containing, so I surmised, a rough facsimile
of me in miniature and Bondo on a swivel base.
I punched it into the front seat, myself in after.
Got back to SR-14 somehow, convulsed with laughter,
but couldn't take the 58 turn-off, because I couldn't turn!
In fact, the foam had taken over and made itself at home.
I couldn't breathe or brake, I couldn't reach the clutch,
couldn't lift the pedal off the floor. I couldn't see out much.
   Rolled to a stop at five past ten, close by a town called Haiwee
or Dove of Peace, remembered for the Owens Valley War
but not the best place for your fuel tank to read empty —
the name is all that's left; the town's a reservoir.
My Haiwee night was long and cold; the foam, thankfully, warm!
The thought did cross my mind I'd erred not filling out that form!
   And now, to nip a long-stemmed saga in the bud
lest the stem be twisted and the rose misunderstood,
the Jaws-of-Life folks pried me loose and ferried me uphill.
And — without so much as asking — dropped off the block of foam.
   Which *did* contain the promised statue, after all —
a perfect likeness, every crease and crack and button,
my spittin' image inside-out, all scrunched up in terror
like the plaster cast they dug up at Pompeii —
you know the one — the Mule Driver Gasping for Air?

Complaint for Breach of Duty to Disclose (May, 2016)

My back yard sits smack in the middle
of the town's busiest flight path.
A flock of blackbirds usurps my airspace
daily disturbs my studious peace,
obscures my view of tree and mountain
like a fountain or a geyser
splashing black ink into my eyes
or like a school of panicked black sardines.
Like frothing Flickas coursing the track
in clock to counterclockwise races,
like CPAs chasing the underground
(I can almost see their bird briefcases)
like blackclad Hasidim in Borough Park
hurrying to shul in the predawn dark.
like tadpoles in a teeming pool
headlong they gush like black
smoke from a locomotive stack.
    None of this was ever disclosed
to me before escrow closed.
    Back and forth in boustrophedic streams
now in Hebrew, now in Greek they scrawl
their cryptographic chronicles.
Like a referee for featherball
I watch these winged black featherballs
eyes trailing them all day long
stretched out on my chaise longue.
Impossible to work this way.
Impossible to read or think
with blackbirds whizzing to and fro all day.
    Not that this pendulum
of feathers in equipoise
pollutes my quiet with stage-4 noise
or that its period annoys or makes me dizzy -
it's just that those black birds are so . . .
so incontinently beautiful —
and busy!

On Granados's "Quejas, o La Maja y el Ruiseñor" (April 14, 2016)
For Brianna Brubaker

Enrique Granados wrote a beautiful piece called "Quejas, o la Maja y el Ruiseñor". The piece is usually described as a dialogue between a young woman and a nightingale. But why is the main title "Complaints"? So far as I know, no one has addressed this question. I love this piece by Granados. The composer must be thinking about the woman he loves, who happens to be enchanted with the song of the nightingale. But Granados, too, has serenaded her with beautiful songs. The woman appreciates them, but cannot hear the difference between his songs and the bird's. His songs are inspired by passion, while his rival is only expressing its longing to be free. Its song has nothing to do with the girl. The composer is bleeding out his life in song for the woman he loves, but it is the lament of the imprisoned nightingale that enraptures her. Hence the plaintive character of this wonderful music!

There is a poem about a maiden pale
who loves to listen to the nightingale.
The bird sings beautifully inside his cage
a mix of music and sweet persiflage.
The girl daydreams the bird sings just for her,
that she is queen, the bird, her courtier.
'Tis but of cloud and wind and sky he sings,
of vistas spreading wide beneath his wings,
sings loud and sweet to bring a mate from far
whom, when she comes, his cage shall only bar.
    How strange that people say that poem's of love
between a maiden and a bird of mauve!
The poet wrote that poem for her. She heard,
and turned away to listen to the bird.

Answering my Mother's Question after Many Years (May 19 [?] – 23, 2016)

When I was just a tiny *feu follet*
you said I'd cry at setting of the sun
as if I thought it would not rise again —
an infant raging at the close of day!
You'd hold me in your arms and ask me why —
as if I knew or even could reply.

The sun has risen many times since then
and now I read astronomy for fun
(though something in me cries even today
on seeing the light grow dim, the setting sun).
I've taught myself to use an astrolabe.
I've read about the photons' dual existence
and how they cook for eons inside the sun
before they surface and reveal their source;
I've read of "spooky action at a distance"
learned much I did not know when a mere babe.
And yet, as pleasant as it is to drown
one's loneliness in smiling seas of learning,
and yet, contented as the day when done,
as lovely as the full moon at half-light,
as ravishing as runes of stars at night,
as sweet the solace of the coming morn,
I still can feel the phantom of my grieving
for the light, a faint twinge of remorse
as for a promise broken, a *ketuba* torn.
    I wonder about that mythic tree of knowledge
growing in the garden of the waking man,
its branches holding out untried temptation
its fruit winking seductively through foliage
of innocent, innocuous delight.
Was it worth that first ecstatic, stolen bite?
    The glory that is man and oh, the horror!
It seems the scales still teeter on the fulcrum.
How long, O Father, until it be resolved?
How long until one pan preponderate?
Or didst Thou, Master of the Universe,
didst Thou foresee or even meditate
the sheer immensity of suffering
that permeates all — nay, *defines* — all being?
I look up heavenward and wait and wait . . .
    And yet the answer is written there in fire
so hot, imagination turns to vapor
from unimaginably far away.
Do you not see it? Look! Look up! Look there!

They seem so cool and tranquil, do they not?
Like the city's vast expanse viewed from the hills,
a sea of diamonds on the clearest summer night.
Those jewels, I think, tell much that is not light!
A vast expanse of thermonuclear wrath
that rips apart the body of primal matter
and rends the very cloth of empty space
still shrieking out the birth pangs of Creation!

    Somewhere therein lies why I wept to see
transparent night succeed translucent day.
That light was rarest, delicatest fruit —
pure reason wrenched from agony and rage;
intuition sweated from black holes;
compassion progeny of lust and passion;
pure love distilled from instinct to survive.

    Can it be an infant's innocent blue eyes
can understand what grownups have forgot?
Unable to articulate, it cries;
a mother hears and tries to soothe the tears.

    It took me seventy long years to say it
and now I have. Bless God and all His work
for it is good and shall endure forever;
and bless mankind, for his work is far from done!

On the Relationship between Mathematics and Madness
(May 29 - 31, 2016)

René Descartes, the inventor of Cartesian coordinates, on which modern trigonometry is based, is considered one of the founders of the 17th-Century Enlightenment Movement—the triumph of rationality over the dreams, dogmas and elixirs of the Renaissance. Descartes postulated that all matter, action, speech and thought could be meaningfully expressed in the common language of numbers. This is not madness? True, but madness nevertheless! Perhaps it was fortunate that he died of pneumonia before he could go completely insane. Others were not so lucky: Georg Cantor, Kurt Gödel, Alan Turing, John Nash—all mathematicians of the highest order. Bertrand Russell never quite made it to full-fledged nuthood, but he did drive one of his sons completely crazy. This phenomenon has given rise to a controversy: does math breed madness, or the other way around? My outdoor musings on that subject gave rise, unexpectedly, to the following:

I saw a dark shadow creep over the hills
I knew what it was, but it gave me the chills —
a fluffy white cloud between earth and the sun
and it scared me so much that I started to run.
For the shadow had turned and was making for me.
But then I stopped running, for where should I flee?
Now the shadow was small and surrounded with light,
yet I stood there immobile, so great was my fright.
Then a messenger came with a crisp telegram.
It said, "Think! [Signed] René," and I knew that I am.
The shadow soon passed, the hills baked in the glare;
though I scoured the landscape, I no longer was there.
Are you wond'ring if I floated off in that cloud,
or perhaps woke up sweating and screaming out loud?
Well, the hills were all sunshine, no clouds were in sight.
I ate a good breakfast with good appetite,
and later that morning, while sipping my tea,
I reviewed my Cartesian *Trigonometrie*.
I am writing these lines from a spa called Bellevue.
I get plenty of rest, got a room with a view —
from where I watch shadows at play in the hills —
but without the anxiety (must be these pills).
The guests are all weird, but quite nice in their way;
and I just got a card: "Get well soon! Yours, René."

Russell's Teapot (June 5-7, 2016)

Bertrand Russell (1872 - 1970) tried to construct a logical system of thought in which every statement would be founded on an irreducible proof. He believed such a system was inconsistent with a belief in God, because, he claimed, there was no evidence that God existed. Somewhat unphilosophically, he compared belief in God to belief in a teapot in orbit around the sun: you can claim it's there, but it can't be proved, and therefore it need not be disproved by those who choose not to believe it. Richard Dawkins has brewed much tea from Russell's pot.

Ironically, however, in his Philosophy, Russell begins his exposition by calling into question whether our thoughts and perceptions correlate to some exterior reality. If they do not, then our sense of "reality" is purely illusory. Since it is impossible, he concedes, to prove that our perception of the world is actually connected to some external reality, we are forced to accept reality as a given, and build from there.

Curiously, Russell appears to have overlooked (I believe deliberately) a fairly simple proof of an external reality to which our minds are connected via the five senses. Indeed, if there is no such reality, where do our perceptions and sensations come from? This question is a valid argument by reductio ad absurdum, *which, formally speaking, should have been enough to lay a logical foundation for Russell's system. I propose that Russell did not want to ask that particular question, because it evokes an uncomfortable answer: the postulate of a God Source of all Percepts, whether mediated by an external reality or not. Better to leave unresolved the question of reality than entertain the possibility of a logical need for a God!*

There is a teapot orbiting somewhere
between Earth and Mars. True! Russell put it there!

Just why he put it there, or what it's brewing
are questions I have recently been chewing.

It isn't tea that's steeping in that pot
but Russell's dormouse (Dawkins), likely as not.

So many Dawkins books are on the shelf,
so simple it can't be to create oneself!

In fact, one might well say, it sort of looks
as though the "Watchmaker" wrote Dawkins' books!

The teapot argument is deeply flawed
if what it's meant to do is refute God.

Is there a church or mosque or shrine or temple
to the Twinings and the Tetleys of your example?

Your captious argument *a dissimilibus*
cannot produce analogy or syllabus.

Confine God to "an eight-by-twelve-foot four-bit
room," before you drink your tea in orbit! *

The eye unto itself is always blind.
Can you prove the World exists, or the Human Mind?

Russell tried but did not push the proof
when he saw the World and God are warp and woof

stretched on a frame of living Human Consciousness.
He turned that loom into a cross of Pontiusness

by making it consist of stuff and logic,
washing his hands of all that's anagogic.

For Russell could have used classic *reductio*
to prove the World was real; cheers and good luck to you

* *From Roger Miller's hit song, "King of the Road".*

if real it isn't! For then, what is the origin
of the oats and bowl we seem to put our porridge in?

Hence, as to reality, he hemmed and hawed
rather than weave an argument for God.

Bert takes the World as given; the rest he ignores:
He's got his pot. His cup is cracked. Who pours?

To make a tea party, you need a trinity:
the World, the Mind and some abstract Divinity!

Each part resists disproof and proof by man.
Now brew *that* in your teapot if you can!

I Love the Spider (November 24-28, 2016) After Victor Hugo

I love the spider and the lowly nettle
because you all consider them a blight
and no indulgence can exhaust or settle —
and everything reproves — their appetite;

because spiders are miserable, unholy
black, disgusting, busy, crawling things
preoccupied with thoughts of themselves solely
yet prisoners of their own ensnaring strings;

because, indifferent to all care and labor
the nettle bids you extend your hand and take;
because the spider poses as your neighbor;
because the nettle's like a garter snake;

because their fame spooks proper citizens
and makes their hand recoil in sudden fright;
because they're both despised as denizens
of damp and rot and vapors of the night.

Stop shuddering! Say grace for the obscure
rejected animal, neglected herb,
for they are humble, bashful and demure
and will not sting if you will not disturb!

Before you crush or slash, remember this:
There is no perfumed rose without its thorn.
Who knows but that the nettle longs to kiss
or that the cellared spider weeps for morn?

Sometimes, when I unconsciously pass near them
on a moonless night, the twinkling stars above me,
and all around is quiet, I think I hear them
pleading softly in the darkness, "Love me!"

What the Torah Doesn't Tell Us (December 11-12, 2016)

And after a year, came to rest
Noah's Ark on Mount Ararat's crest.
No sign of the Flood
but some puddles of mud —
into which Noah's kids jumped fully dressed!

Thoughts from a Leather Couch (January 23-24, 2017
Revised, Oct. 7, 2017)

. . . yet come to think of it, there is another
reason — one I hesitate to share
with anybody — least of all, my mother,
lest I give her a fright by laying it bare.
It's not that I remember something now
I didn't then, nor is it that I lied,
exactly; it's just that I have always known —
or felt — that I was born the day I died;
and that I died after the sun went down —
can't say that I recall exactly how.
I do remember blood — the bloodred sun.
I can't undo the things I saw being done.
I can't forget what kills me to remember.
I can't *yohrtzeit* my birthday next November . . .

Q & A (June 7, 2017)

Conches of Consciousness!
Cogs of Cognition!
Ethanols of Ethics!
Eczemas of Existence!

I like to watch philosophers
performing autopsies, autos da fé
on imaginary oranges, onions, melons.

It isn't I who would have asked their questions
nor do I have a yen to bite into their answers.
But I do enjoy it when I read them
raptly peeling away the rind, the layers
earnestly dissecting and proportioning out
the fruit, the bulb, the portly pepo
scooping out the pulp of moral remorations.
There's always some lost juice or sweat or mush
for jugglers in the wings or acrobats to wipe up
while swinging from their high IQs with ease
or from their logically EQ'd trapeze
ropes moored to the clouds
nets anchored to the clowns.

I learned early on not to ask too many questions.
"Why does the sun shine?" "To dry up the rain."
"Why does it rain?" "So flowers don't dry up in the sun."
"Why do dogs howl at the moon?"
"To answer other dogs howling at the earth."

 All the great Answers are the same as these —
the ones I got from Mom and Dad.
Or perhaps not quite as good.
All the answers are given, already out there.
"Blowin' in the wind," as Bob Dylan put it.
All you have to do is ask.
But why, when you and I both know,
since Socrates and Plato,
philosophers cut questions to fit their answers
much as tailors cut clothes for customers.
Which is no crime: customers can't very well go naked —

not since those first rum customers slipped —
and good shmattes, like good questions, shouldn't go to waste.

If haberdashers make their livelihood
in spite of baseball cap and hood,
couturiers may also eat — and eat, they should!
They wield the scissors, ply the subtle needles
sprinkle the multicolored sequins
like yentes making matches on the phone
fitting cloth to truth and truth to cloth
while Truth, the spinster, reads Harlequins
and watches *Home Alone.*

Which begs the question: Are answers beggars
and questions, perhaps, choosers?
I don't see thinkers as bootleggers
or students of philosophy as boozers.

On the other hand, I'm not afraid of chaos
don't need to sort the universe like socks
or see diamonds in the Brownian rough.
Physics, math and Mozart are enough
sipped with some jiggling molecules of tea
a cube of sugar for philosophy,
a poem for my sweet tooth.
Just think of me as content to sleuth
the trail that leads from God to Guess?
(via Pucci, Ricci and Madame Grès)
clad in a loincloth of Depends —
if only to spite popular trends.

Not that I consider Truth an aerosol
or an unknown *inconnu* at Place de l'Étoile
nor will you find her in the Place Pigalle
or at a Motel Six with the light turned off and all
or in the archives of Interpol
or in the offices of City Hall.
Nor will you see her on the Mall
inside the Lincoln Memorial
or the Rotunda of the Capitol.
Nor will she be caught in mid pratfall
while circusgoers clap and LOL.

She walks a trail of tears
a trail of chickens and of eggs
on which one egg is always left unhatched
like a marker egg marked with an "X"
one answer widowed and unattached.

Look! Here's a potato
left unpeeled by Plato!
Dare we peel it?
Vladimir Ilyitch: *Chto Delat?*
Look! There's an egg the *Federalist*
stargazers missed!
Tom, Alex, Jim and John:
What is to be Done
when Philosophy goes for a gun?
If you know the answer, anyone,
please copyright it and reveal it!
Here's what I say: Run, man, run!

Dead or Alive (July 7 - 18, 2016)

It's been quite a few years since I've stopped growing.
I've lost an inch or two from age and drought.
My nails and hair continue to grow out,
although the rest of me seems to be slowing.

It saddens me to think that so much glory
should end in buzz and manicure and shave.
I'm told that nails and hair grow in the grave
which makes of mine a live *memento mori*.

Or else, perhaps I *am* already dead.
But if I'm dead, death can't be a full stop
if I can nonetheless grow such a crop
while treading water where I cast my bread,

and doing my own hard time, and taking five
to write a deadbeat novel or dead letter.
And if I'm *not* dead, well, so much the better:
I have all the perks of death — *plus I'm alive!*

Reprieve (February 2-3, 2016)

> " . . . if design govern in a thing so small."
> —Robert Frost

A spider saw me coming
(big and ugly!)
and skittered to a corner
where my instinct was
to crush it with my boot.
Why I didn't, I don't know.
Perhaps its resignation stayed my foot
or its Creator
wrapped me like a fly
in the fine webwork of His will.
Whichever — the arachnid or the One —
it eyed me from below
with its 8-ball eyes,
and quivering in its knees
cowered in its corner
till I passed from the room.
Later I saw it make a beeline toward my bed.
My instinct was to kill it —
enough said.
    It isn't guilt that nags me now
although I feel that creepy thing
deserved to live
by virtue of its secret purpose
(perhaps to save a king
half-hidden in a cave)
but the odd meaning
of those intervening hours
that gave it time
ostensibly to weave a note
and put its small affairs in order.

Ravens and Rooklets (March 9-11, 2016)

I saw ravens and rooklets wheeling madly
in the whirling whiteness of the snowflakes swirling
even as the fallen flakes were pearling
on the window warm from my breath, rolling sadly

down glass and intermeddling with the passing
of light from black and white and wing and flake
just at a time when so much was at stake
between crystal and feather, melt and massing

so that I still don't know who won the fight
or what the brouhaha was all about
now that all's quiet and the sun's come out
and the sky's alive with black, the earth with white —

unless the scene was pure delight and laughter
birds chasing snowflakes as I chase a thought
but having nought to do with battles fought
inside the soul for the unfathomable hereafter.

Dord, a Soliloquy (August 11, 2016; Revised August 14, 2017)
Imagine this as a monolog addressed to a bartender who pretends to be listening.

Big dictionaries
ponderous, imperious,
pedantic, autocratic.
Webster's Second would have rowed for Yale
but for its corpulence.
Wore spectacles, smoked pipes.
The OED attended Oxford U.
Won't ever let you forget it.
Got my awesome Second from the discard pile;
my Oxford for five bucks.
Had to join Book of the Month.
I quit after a Month. None of their books
called for a dictionary — let alone the OED.
Now Webster's wears a combover,

compensates for weightloss surgery
with inflated print.
Oxford English looked sent down
when it arrived, crestfallen
subdued as if it had gone through
the Freudian meatgrinder.
Split right down the middle
between making ozyat
and minding your Ps and Qs.
Ego shrunk to microprint —
twelve tomes of id squashed down to two.
Neatly encased, compartmentalized
it came with an optimistic lens.
That didn't help my friend Tom Lynch
find his, lost on the road while hitchhiking
to Del Rio to meet the Wolfman.
Webster's got a critical shellacking,
skulks in hall lockers
under a dying ham sandwich or a pair of living socks,
sulks in highschool libraries
ruminating words
that don't belong in dictionaries,
things that can't be put into words.
The dord of dictionaries
the fate of nations:
destiny or density.
It's all in how you dord the letters.
The dord of order or disorder.
The Oweedee still wears a Bobby's helmet
still struts unarmed
among Masters candidates
and aspiring novelists.
I hear the next edition of M-W
will rehabilitate "dord"
(a perfectly good word
in my sober estimation)
and come with a 3-D-printed assault rifle.
Somewhere maybe in Connecticut
a college prof still drawls the bizarre tale
of how he became an English major.

Reality Check (August 12-14, 2016) for Steven Rudin and Penny
According to research, olfactory dreams are extremely rare.

I dreamed it rained, or so it dimly seemed
but though I dreamed and heard the raindrops fall
I thought perhaps it was the rain that dreamed
for when I woke, and long lay dreaming there,
it seemed as if it hadn't rained at all

and as I listened for the pitter patter
the gurgle and the chatter of the water
I wondered at the play of mind and matter
and whether rain or drain I couldn't tell —
until I leaned outside and smelled the air
the smell of streets and sidewalks wet and gleaming
and only then I knew I wasn't dreaming.

I think the rain wonders at this as well:
Do rains have dreams?
Do dreams come from rain showers?
That's why I think rain falls — to smell the flowers.

The Ant and the Lion (September 18, 2016)

The shadow of an ant at setting sun
is longer than a lion's at high noon.

Rainbow Witness (September 26 - October 21, 2016)

A Jew is not supposed to gaze at rainbows!
But this one hung so brilliant and straight ahead,
the freeway like an arrow for three, four miles . . .
    It is a law that harks back to the Flood
the great deluge, Noah's Ark, the dove,
the raven and the rainbow . . .
    When a King unscrolls before your eyes
the document of your reprieve
you do not attempt to read!
    Yet there in front of me,
in blazing technicolor, a double arc —
an arch more than an arc —

tangible, electric, as though to walk in it
your hairs would stand on end,
your clothes would crackle.
    The strange thing is it did not move.
Although a rainbow is but reflection and refraction
(illusion conjured up by mist and light,
the angle of the eye subtended by the sun,
described by higher math)
and should recede as you advance,
it stood its ground unmovable, defiant
demeanor architectural
not meteorological
yet not of stainless steel
standing aside obsequiously
to let the Mississippi pass,
not lofting freight trains over a grand crevasse
but like a living monument
astride a stream of consciousness.
    As I drew near it seemed to rear and swell
until it towered like a citadel
so firm and resolute that when I drove through
I looked for the obverse in the rearview.
    And there was none.
Saw nothing but a setting sun
a long road unspooling in a mirror —
not one reflecting in reverse
but more like a parauniverse
in which all things were just the same
except I lived and went by a different name.

The Lens Grinder (December 5, 2016)

The wind polishes
the water's surface
like an old lens grinder
or a young philosopher.
The wind too is an outcast
spinning the weathercocks for direction.

Roll the dice.
There is a board game above the weather.
Hard to know which way the wind is blowing.
Yet when the wind is still
the water gleams and shines
like the lens of a telescope.
Strive my soul to be like water
because the way is lost to me.
I have not learned to read the heavens.
There is a blind spot over the north star.
The sun annihilates the eye.
We must note where it sets and whence it rises.
We will deduce by shadows
infer the compass in the morning
circumference the time.
Let us blaze a new trail with heart and mind.
No use standing on your head.
When lights glimmer from below
you have to know you are above the stars.

Driving up the Mountain in a Thick Fog (January 11, 2017)

    This fog had no cat feet. All mouth, it swallowed me —
the kind of fog that caused a massive pile-up
in the Central Valley on the ninety-nine
ten years ago. I think the toll was grim,
their visibility twenty times mine,
and I'm going up a mountain, driving blind!
Doing twenty on the freeway, maybe slower.
It's one AM. Can't see ten feet ahead.
Can just make out a pair of lights behind.
The thought he can't see mine fills me with dread.
Must be that 18-wheeler, the one that followed me
onto the northbound ramp. About a mile up,
just when the miasma can't get more opaque,
he closes fast, swings out to overtake

me, roars into the soup. "That man's insane!"
I shout. But then he slows into my lane.
I realize what he's doing, and follow him.
The ascent's three times as long — almost an hour.
Reaching the summit, I can't see the town.
I have to highbeam every passing sign.
MILL STREET 1 MILE. I breathe. I signal right.
His blinker echoes mine. I follow down
the ramp and over the bridge. The town's a blackout.
Now he turns left. I tail him still, but back out
quick, my words of blessing in my mouth.
I saw it just in time: he's heading south!

Forelius Pusillus (January 29-30, 2017)

I saw two ants, let's call them Ned and Fred,
dragging an insect larva to their nest
I assume the nest, assume the larva dead,
but note the naked facts re all the rest:

Ned held one end, Fred held the other.
Enthralled by their cooperative enterprise,
I knelt to observe more closely, when another
ant approached more than three times their size.

The smaller pair commenced evasive action,
each alternately halting and advancing,
both jointly feinting and changing direction
so that you'd think the two of them were dancing.

The intruder did not seem at all impressed
by such quaint tactics, and kept up his harrying,
till maybe Fred — or was it Ned? — hard pressed,
released the carcass' end that he was carrying,

and turned to face the formidable foe!
The fight was brief, the outcome was foregone.
He reared to strike and was cut clean in two,
as though in chess one sacrificed a pawn.

I saw this drama with my own two eyes.
So stunned was I by what I saw, I can't
even recall what happened to the prize.
Fred ran, as would have I, were I an ant.

The question left behind, however, is this:
The actions of both Fred and Ned implied
communication and analysis —
stratagems conjointly thought and tried.

First, how did Fred and Ned cooperate
to lift the carcass like two men, a couch?
How did the two of them coordinate
response to their antagonist's approach?

How did the pair deliberate as one
to begin diversion when evasion failed?
What made them choose to resist rather than run?
Did they not know the risk a fight entailed?

And most of all, how did those mites decide
which one of them was more, which less, expendable,
push come to shove, in case one of them died?
At such a pass, are pheromones dependable?

New Science posits altruistic genes;
but Ned's and Fred's are more than altruistic
since their behavior indicates some means
anthropomorphically rationalistic!

Now why have I set forth this droll account
if not to show that poetry and science
may issue from the selfsame source or fount—
be it so humble as observing my ants?

For it seems that when a scientist shuts an eye
to observations that don't fit the scheme,
a poet must not hesitate to defy
convention and cross over the mainstream.

There is an ant, endemic to Brazil,
the entrance to whose nest is sealed at night
by a few outcasts subservient to some will
that shuts them out indifferent to their plight.

Of those ejected very few survive!
Who knows but that their need to leave the nest
is so much greater than their need to live
that in their dying they know that they are blest?

Bless God who made His world so full of wonder;
so full of splendid beings each with its reason!
Walk carefully, that you not tread them under,
Rachmana Litzlan, Kyrie Eleison!

How Are You? (Jan. 22-23, 2017)

I am, Bless God, OK.
My complaints are to Hashem.
He answers with complaints about me.
What do I complain about to Hashem?
That He doesn't bake my *challos*.
What does He complain about to me?
That my oven isn't hot enough.
Is this not enough like marriage?
Bless God, I am OK.

La Bellissima Biondina (February 23-24, 2017)
(After listening to Liszt's "Venezia e Napoli", as played by Jeno Jando)

Now turn your mind's eye to the *Serenissima*,
your mind's ear to the boatman's ardent song —
a song sung to a youth and his *bellissima*,
while beneath the oar the gondola glides along.

The truth is that the ancient gondolier
sings not to them, but sings for her alone;
the lad has no suspicion that the tear
shed by the girl is for the old *vecchione*.

No word must pass between him and the lass.
No look, no sign can ever be exchanged
between the two of them. They know, alas,
what is, what was, that nothing can be changed.

And yet, beneath their feet, the current flows,
the water changing with the changing light,
the dipping oar, the lapping wave repose
the soul, and lovers make a pleasing sight.

A Woman You Have Loved (March 12-22, 2017)

A woman you have loved never grows old;
never shall die the memory of her beauty.
Not so the man, or so I'm lately told.
Alas, he lacks, she has, no sense of duty.

Some say it is the other way around:
that female is the faithful, male the fickle;
that women unloved, betrayed, stay duty-bound;
that love, for men, is just an itch they tickle.

Thinking back upon the girls I've dated,
I wonder why it is so complicated,
when mourning doves remain forever mated.

Or why, when I awoke one lazy morning,
thinking of her beauty still adorning,
my dove forever mated me to mourning.

The Ancestry of Flowers (June 26 – July 25, 2017)

The ancestry of flowers is hard to ascertain.
Man leaves a bone; trees turn to stone.
But when a flower dies, few memories remain —
memories like candles in the rain.

Yet all things come from something; nothing stays the same.
The rivers flow, and where they go,
lay down alluvia of legend, lore and fame —
ancestors of long-forgotten name.

Yet flowers do possess an ancient ancestry;
and this I heard from a hummingbird
who built a nest high in a venerable plum tree —
plums that bear sweet taste of memory.

Before Adam and Eve, he said, there was a race
of lotus men, much like children,
endowed with great intelligence and charm and grace,
graceful of form and beautiful of face.

Only, their beauty, skin deep, led them to adore
beyond all measure the ideal of pleasure.
Shallow as the sea slides up the slanting shore,
pleasure itself became their *Baal Peor*.

Disdaining ancient vows, they liberalized the laws;
preferred to rove for perfect love
instead of laboring to alleviate the flaws;
forever looking for the exit clause.

To abolish hate, they warped those whom they ought protect.
They used their schools to impose new rules
behind closed classroom doors, and useless to object!
Yet violence continued on unchecked.

And every fall, young scholars to their schools returning,
within their breasts, standardized tests
choked intellectual thirst, put out the fire burning,
failed to impart a love for books and learning.

Instead, their garden, sown and overgrown with weeds
choked rhyme and reason (out of season),
the vacant freedom empty education breeds
leading to all manner of foul misdeeds!

Their government passed laws promoting euthanasia,
infanticide and suicide,
abolished bail, enacted bills for a Fantasia —
symptoms of Carl Wernicke's aphasia.

A false promise of happiness, all would pursue it;
preached-to on spirit, refuse to hear it.
The motto on their bills was "*Coitibus Annuit*."
Sex became a lax exchange of fluid,

a constant and obsessive topic of discussion
like heavy metal in the parietal
with consequential hemicranial percussion,
flashing lights, convulsions of blue Prussian.

Until God said, "I miss the songs of birds and bees
and brooks, the sough of winds. Enough!"
and with a wave changed profligates to peonies,
violets white, and wood anemones.

And God surveyed His work, and He declared it good;
erased the shame of the ill fame
left by the libertines in every field and wood
and planted blooms where lotus folk had stood;

and fixed their sexual parts where their loose tongues had been —
just retribution for the pollution
everywhere they'd spread with love's unholy twin.
Oh give me bowls to put some flowers in!

Oh let me look on them and contemplate the crust
of bitter years through bitter tears
yet see fresh beauty born amid their very dust,
at least to die with one last living thrust!

The ancestry of flowers is hard to ascertain.
Man leaves a bone; trees turn to stone.
But when a flower dies, few memories remain —
memories like candles in the rain.

Echein kai ouk Echein (2017) To Stamatis Philippides

I console myself with this, alas:
that where I live is like Hellás.
Not that I have what you have got,
but that I don't what you have not.

A Bee in Switzerland (June 4-5, 2017)
To Esther Hadassah

Sometimes I feel I have to hug my head.
It's one of just three places I can hug
myself: my head, my knees, and, if I shrug,
my shoulders. Still, not you, but me instead.

I can embrace my knees when lying in bed
or sitting on the grass watching a bug
or talking to my cat stretched on the rug;
but not *your* knees, my worried, muddled head

upon your lap; can't hug my feet (Rimbaud,
bent over his dilapidated shoe!)
nor my behind, as I learned years ago

in Switzerland, when I sat on a bee.
But I can hug my head, though full of you,
when I hear you cry out, "My Love! Hug me!"

Black Coffee Blues (October 22, 2017)

I have a problem with the Starbucks team.
I say, "I'll have a coffee. I'd like it black."
Could be LA or Flint or Hackensack,
they will reply, "Shall I leave room for cream?"

It drives me mad and makes we want to scream.
And they don't like it when I answer back,
"Did you not hear me say I want it black?"
They hiss when I come in, "Oh no, it's him!"

I had a dream last night and in this dream
I go to Starbucks and I ask for cream.
The girl salutes as though I were an officer

and smiling, asks, "Shall I leave room for coffee, Sir?
"Yes please," I say. "Now, kindly hold the cream,
and fill the cup with coffee: to the brim!"

A Matter of Perspective (June 19, 2017)

July 20, 1969, a human being
first set foot on the moon.
June 12, 2017, a black widow spider
first set foot on Brown County, Wisconsin.
One small step for a spider.
One giant leap for a man.

Kites (July 19-25, 2017)

A boy, a breeze, a kite.
An old man, a thought, a pen to write.

This three of things —
a trine conjoined by twine,
a poet inspired by a little wine.

Substance, mind, opposing force
keep the kite aloft,
the poem on course.

I flew kites as a small boy
but did not see my kite
as writing on a page of sky.

Now I see the two are of a kind
when, writing verse, I find
myself being lifted by the wind.

The Institute of Anguish (October 27, 2017)

Somewhere there is an Institute of Anguish
where whitecoated men conduct clinical trials
and in- and out-patients convulse or languish
while pretty nurses dispense cool, clinical smiles.

The pain is part of a covert experiment
to test the farthest limits of humanity
inside a self-contained, controlled environment
and map the road from sanity to insanity.

When the enterprise had dug through all the strata,
its purpose changed to self-perpetuation.
Invoking the enormity of data,
the Institute raised funds for renovation!

So now the site's a shrine, and, daily, pilgrims
come, prepared with craven immorality
to gape at the Zimbardos and the Milgrams,
and overlook the Eichmanns! In reality,

the data were all compiled eons ago,
but the cries, the screams, the anguish, on they go!

A Falling Leaf (November 16 - 29, 2017)
In Memory of Esther Hadassah Optican

I was inspired to write the following stanzas by the Scherzo movement of Mendelssohn's miraculous Opus 20, which was in turn inspired by the following stanza from Goethe's Faust:

>   Wolkenzug und Nebelflor
>   Erhellen sich von oben
> Luft im Laub, und Wind im Rohr,
>   – Und alles ist zerstoben.

>   Trails of cloud and mist
>   Brighten from above;
> Breeze in the trees, and wind in the reeds,
>   – And all is scattered.

December, and the leaves turned gold and brown.
One of them prayed "Don't let me be forgotten!"
Its plea reached Heaven as it floated down
and came to rest on the earth, compressed and trodden.

In its descent, it had described an arc
as graceful as a dancer's pirouette,
and beautiful as the ascending lark
or a movement of young Mendelssohn's Octet.

   The soul that sees, the leaf that falls must plead
for life and beauty to endure forever!
Whence cometh that desire, whence the need —
if not to make bland beauty blaze or shiver?

The joys of life, the ecstasies of beauty
draw nourishment from their impermanence
to intensify our praise, as is our duty,
straying in the wilderness, dwelling in tents.

   Three hundred million years or more have passed:
a lump of coal imprinted with a leaf
is found — as if to prove such things do last.
And yet the memory itself is brief —

brief as the burning of, or as long buried
preserved in dark — and so preserved for whom?
Oft have I wondered, seldom have I queried:
When memories perish, how preserve the tomb?

Long pondered the Creator this enigma,
desiring to confer on His Creation
of life the sting, of ecstasy the stigma,
wherewith to whet mankind for Revelation:

   "Unwillingly though I forbear to make
immortal life and beauty for this sphere,
I must withhold My hand for My own sake;
yet will I multiply, piled tier on tier,

both life and beauty like crystals of snow
on warm, black wool, like stars on cold, black night,
to melt or blow apart, an overflow
of unrepeated song all sung at sight.

But this I swear: nothing of what must perish
shall be forgot but evil, which be banished!
For what I have created I will cherish
unto the day when everything is vanished.

Then will I rest once more and meditate
and soothe Myself. For I shall suffer more
than all their sufferings. Then shall I create
new worlds, perhaps, and better than before!"

   Now these were not God's words, to be exact,
but mine. And He Who placed them in my heart
did so as poetry, and not as fact.
And yet they echo more with truth than art.

   Just this I'd ask, if I were Abraham:
Is't right the innocent of man and beast
should suffer like the wicked of Sodom?
Does *Thy* pain quiet *their* pain in the least?

   And then spoke God to this unworthy mite:
"Now was it I who killed Cain's brother, Abel?
And should I not have spared him in despite?
Was I too soft at the revolt of Babel?

When I sent rain to cleanse the earth from blood
and set my hopes upon the righteous Noah
that human beings might claim descent from Good,
was it for Hiroshima or the Shoah?

How many Holocausts have I prevented?
How many have I freed that were enslaved?
How often has Vesuvius relented?
How many roads to hell have I unpaved?

But this you cannot know and can't foresee.
For I disguise My Mercy with misfortune —
My Lovingkindness with catastrophe,
lest man besiege My Justice, and importune.

For if My Mercy were plainly revealed,
My Lovingkindness known but by the half,
the universe would quickly come unsealed
and nations revel round a golden calf.

   And have I not conferred on man My Law,
without which wrong were right and worse were better,
darkness My perfection, light My flaw,
the alphabet composed of one mute letter?

   My choice in making man was plainly this:
Shall I make Adam one and make him God?
Or, as I have explained in Genesis,
make him a multitude, mortal and flawed?

The 'flaw' in My creation is Free Will,
which I bestowed on man to be My foil.
And man being many, he must strive until
unto My statutes he cleave true and loyal.

   True, death brings fear, despair and grief and sorrow —
also Repentance. Faith and love console,
and waken promise of a brighter morrow
and the inner sense of one's immortal soul.

   Now why would you nudge Father Abraham
to question Me and e'en take Me to task?
The answers I just placed into your palm
he knew full well, and hence he didn't ask!

For like unto your leaves are human lives.
And part of man is mortal animal.
When spring returns, the barren tree revives.
The tree is man and man grows wise withal."

   The autumn leaves carpet the ground with gold,
but every last one living, strange to tell,
clings to a fragile twig as nights grow cold
and mourns the spot where its companion fell.

NON EXPLICIT PAUSA EST

Charlie's Angel (December 2 - 6, 2017)

Shelley Hull was associate producer, with Aaron Spelling, of the TV series, Charlie's Angels.

When I returned from Italy
a wreath around my brow
people made fun of me
mocked me for the Latin and the Greek.
"But what do you *do?*" they asked
underlining the second "do".
Even college deans
disparaged my hardearned degree.
"Laureates aren't worth much here,"
proclaimed one academic snob.
I needed a job.

So I asked Mr. Hull, my father's friend
if he could get me hired.
Shelley worked with Spelling
had all the connections
knew all the ins and outs
joked how they would icecube Farrah before a shoot
to make her nipples stand and salute.

Begging forgiveness, Shelley declined.
"You are too refined," he said,
"for that degenerate milieu.
You'd never fit! You could not survive!
You can't imagine how vulgar these people are
how foul their language
how low their manners.
A scholar and a gentleman like you?
You'd quit or cramp their style
and soon be out on your peristyle!"

Well, now it's all out in the open —
at least some of what he meant —
as BODs phone up the spouse to order in
and don their gloomy robes
to purge the industry
of the more conspicuous pervs —
Brasso the image the shareholder deserves.

The indignities those ladies had to put up with!
The daily gauntlet of innuendo
the sly hands, the invasive tongues
the random quickie drugged or under duress
the surreptitious grabs and gropes
while grinning for the photo ops.

You can't not see the networks posturing and preening
you can't not feel something for the perps.
All those hopeful, pretty young women
actricettes, auditionettes and anchorettes —
from all their cleavages a polytropous pheromone
floods our blood vessels with testosterone.

How can a man keep focused on his work?
How can a guy stand up behind his desk?
"C'mon in! Come in! Please sit down!
Honey, would you like a drink? How 'bout a scotch?"
Jeezus! You can almost see her crotch!

I wasn't aiming for a TV career,
but television I could write!
I could have done research for Xena
I could have written a blue streak —
Hercules and Cleopatra
bickering in ancient Greek.

Ah Sheller, now I capeesh, I understand!
The liquorladen chainsmoking smutswearing
crude participles and puns
the crass quips about flying nuns . . .

If I am not today what you thought I'd be
what would I be if you had gotten me that job?
A bigshot mogul with a hall pass
for patting some young intern's ass?

Or, like you, a decent, harried man
a little too much captive of his role
who still knew when to barricade the pass
and bar the road to Balaam's ass.

Analysis: The Blues (Jan. 21 - 23, 2018)

"The way it used to be, it ain't the same,"
said the old black man to someone.
Or maybe no one. And I don't know
if he meant to quote the song or not,
but the way he said it works for me,
though without the music,
it definitely ain't the same.
"Things ain't what they used to be" is the song.
but what it means, in case you got it wrong,
is things was not so good, but now they gettin' better!
Now my eyes on the far horizon can see a glow
announcin' things ain't what they used to be!
A glow on the horizon, maybe.
Something a white man might not see,
or might see differently.

What is that glow, after all,
that Duke's kid sang about?
A new dawn? A rosy promise?
Reverse nostalgia? Nostalgia for the future?
Africa, maybe? His father's song, *Petite Fleur Africaine*!
Black nostalgia must be rooted far, far back —
Far back and away. You'd think
there wouldn't be too much nostalgia
packed close to home. A lot of bitterness, outrage and rage.
Some hope. A little flower of Africa, maybe?
The Duke could smell that bit of sweet from here.
The way it was in Africa, it's here it ain't the same.

You kinda know what his son was thinking of.
The words aren't his. They come from Simon Schwartz:
the dawn of a day of glory: millennium! —
A Jew thinking of the Redemption!
Got so weary of bein' nothin'. . .
That must be Duke's kid Mercer talkin' —
a little sunshine for a flower in the shade!

I don't know what the other fellow meant,
that old black man I overheard one summer day
on Wilshire Boulevard, L.A.
Maybe just the good ol' times, remembering
the girls, the cadillac, the food Ma made, the jazz.
I like to think all Black folk think of Africa
from time to time as they go place to place.
It ain't there either the way it used to be!

Africa! The Bible says
that's where God made humanity.
But just as hard to find it there
as it is to find it anywhere.
My eyes on the horizon don't see rose.
As for the Redemption, nobody knows
when that's gonna be or how.
Just know it won't be the same as now.

Phonecall (Nov. 7, 2013, revised, expanded, Feb. 10, 2018)

Some woman telephoned me from Mombasa
to say my ex was stranded, and to ask . . .
which set me off — my life, tabula rasa —
a roof, a phone, some bread, an empty flask . . .

"Why scam," I scolded, "when you could get rich
by holding out an honest hand and cup!"
She answered back: "Hey, Sonko, there's the hitch!
An honest beggar rich?" And she hung up.

And suddenly it hit me: honest labor
too, is mixed with fraud, deceit and theft,
your right stretched out to soften up your neighbor
while you contrive to rob him with your left!

The contents of an honest begging bowl
are like just pay for working like a mule —
a little kindness mixed with daily gruel,
and knowing there's nothing in it that you stole.

Time Capsule (February 12, 24, 2018)

Some poets have been encapsulating poems
to send deep into interstellar space.
This speaks not well for them or what they write
or for the investment counselors of the race.
The cost is staggering, returns are small
and even traveling at the speed of song,
the wait for a response is rather long.
Could take a million years for a rocket ship
to get there and another million back —
too long to wait for a rejection slip!

    These poets seem to be implying that life
on earth is not intelligent enough
to appreciate their stuff. To be polite,
we earthlings call that *peeing* into the void.
Bury your poems under a banyan tree:
the odds are better for posterity.

    One time, I dropped a bottle overboard
at midpoint of a transatlantic crossing.
I soon forgot about it. I was ten.
A *buachaill* on a beach happened to spot it.
and wrote me back by ordinary mail.
Four years for the full circuit! The reply:
"I am a poor schoolboy in Doolin, County Clare.
Please send me any money you can spare."

    The strange thing is that forty-four years later,
an Irish poet sent me through his agent
a fey chrestomathy of woe, which I,
for reasons not important here, rejected.
And ever since, the thought that I betrayed
some artifice of irony foreordained
by dramaturgs of fate whines in my brain
like a mosquito in a madman's ear:
"He sent you poems, and you refused to hear!"

Birdwatching (February 21-28, 2018)

The yard is full of little birds;
I watch them as they feed.
They skip and hop from place to place,
their beaks stuffed full with seed.

They cannot see me at my post —
they'd fly off if they did . . .
I wish I could consort with them
but keep myself well hid.

One little fellow left the flock
and went out for a stroll.
Not seeing me, he approached so close,
I nearly lost control!

I'd gladly watch these birds all day
but that my nose is sore
where I slammed my head against the glass
of the sliding patio door.

That Fleeting Shade of Green (March 1-4, 2018)

> *Komm gleich nach dem Sonnenuntergange,*
> *sieh das Abendgrün des Rasengrund;*
>
> — Rilke

I have seen the green the poet sighed.
It is a green that I have seen at eventide
in Umbria — let us call it *perusine* —
an afterhours green that green
in any language doesn't really mean
except as aquarelled by Rilke in light between,
the watercolor running ere the light declines,
to capture in a chaos of titivating lines
the tide of feeling to which the tint gave rise.

He saw that greenish tincture in more northern clime
but both, in Rilke's poem — quattrains and skies —
pale as pink of thistledown, as green of thyme,
revacillant in verse, irresolute in rhyme —
combine to name what green can't signify.
   How can a word capture the what and why
without defining for the unseeing eye
a butterfly pinned to a board nailed to a wall?
Do you see how green becomes a screen withal,
whereas the poem, a distillate of light and gloom
of burdened boughs of orchardappled treen
more real than wood, delectable than fruit, more fresh,
more passionate than love that germinates
and generates and nourishes the flesh?
   Between the meaning and the word —
the words arranged and printed on a page —
between the sunset and the greening of the sward,
betwixt the ecstasy of estrus and the pain,
beyond the word, the bird without the cage,
ecce the essence, the intoxication of the term,
the zephyr of the zygote of the germ
by which to grasp that fleeting shade of green
and fix it to the sky and in the mind
and add it to the dictionary of the blind.

Korach (March 14-16, 2018)

If it rained more often, I'd have seen it sooner.
There's a guy looking up through the puddles.
His face is quizzical, as though he's wondering
about a world that's upside-down.
He sees me standing on my head
feet glued to the ceiling like a fly
and for a moment that's what I think I am —
a fly on the ceiling — and he marvels
that my hat stays on. Inverted fish with wings
perplex him, as do the fires burning under water.

Most days, I never see this man.
He potters under the dry earth looking for a waterhole.
The other day, I went outside.
The sky was waterlogged with clouds.
One of them stuck out its tongue at me
uncurling it like a party whistle
until it touched the ground and beckoned.
It looked like a long white climbing road.
I got into my car and drove toward it.
I had such a yen to drive up it, but got scared and didn't.
As I passed beneath, I heard a roll of thunder from overhead
and looked up just in time to see it lick its lips.
There but for the grace of God . . .
Heading home, I passed an old prospector
by the roadside, doing yoga in the rain
or thumbing for a ride with his big toe.

Resumé (March 21-22, 2018)

Venus aglitter in the east at dawn
a gentian blue upon an Alpine rock
a bloom with one bright bead of light upon
a leaf delicately veined upon its stalk

a single line of quizzic beauty drawn
by Klee or by Picasso, a cube by Braque
a skull with open book by Paul Cézanne
the iris white I wept for by Van Gogh

the afternoon and evening of a faun
the morning after one's true love has gone
a picnic laid for one upon the lawn

the ticking of an old grandfather clock
a rime-encrusted bottle of cognac
a diary in a drawer with rusted lock

Shortcuts (March 4-8, 2018)

A Roman sailed the sea in a caravel
to test the holy Sage, Rabbi Hillel.

"If you can teach me on one leg (not two!)
the entirety of Torah, I'll be a Jew."

Hillel responded, "*Don't do something to
another, you would not want done to you.*

"That is the essence: all the rest is gloss.
Now go and learn! Immerse yourself in *Shas!*" *

   "Give me the kernel, standing on one foot,"
a Jew adjured the preacher in pursuit.

The Christian answered, "*Love thy fellow man –
even thy enemy!* The rest is bran."

"If thus you love me, how am I to know,"
queried the Jew, "if you be friend or foe?"

"That's not my problem," smiled Christian to Jew.
Replied the Jew, "It is, if I love you!"

   A Frenchman asked Hegel to give the sense
of his philosophy in one sentence.

Hegel, complying, wrote ten tomes, thick and dense.**
(They really did comprise one long sentence!)

   An Englishman approached the great Voltaire,
and asked if he could tell him, *pied en l'aire*,

"*Qu'est-ce que ça veut dire, être français?*"
Voltaire replied, "Go ask Mme Châtelet"

(his mistress once, lately of Saint-Lambert).
"*Elle va te l'expliquer* deux *pieds en l'aire!*"

---

* *Shas: Shisha Sedarim*, the Six Orders of the Mishna.
** Will Durant, *The Story of Philosophy* (NY: Simon & Schuster, 1926), p. 320.

178

The Moon Up Close (May 30, 2018)

Poets, particularly the Chinese
bless the moon for its beauty.
We tend to be more cerebral.
We do not wait for the moment of her greatest beauty
the moment when her splendor
showers the heavens and the earth like fireworks.
For us it is enough that she have substance and be visible.
Timing is all important.
Not too early, not too late.

Up close, the moon is not so alluring.
A rather dusty, barren place
if photograph and film are to be believed.
Distance is what airbrushes the moon.
And beauty does require distance.
Or else a great deal of care
with razors, tweezers, powders, paints
and blandishments of candlelight and compliment
a little music perhaps?
A chilled tulip of white wine?

The irony is that landing on the moon
her beauty becomes almost irrelevant.
A mental, not a physical thing.
The focus is on the achievement, *n'est-ce pas?*
It is as though the sense of beauty
surprising the act
retires abashed and awed to a secret hiding place
somewhere in space
awake but cringing,
afraid to breathe, almost.

How Old Am I Now? (Question for an SAT) (June 6, 2018)

An old man made a wish, infirm and lame
and I, 30 years his junior, wished the same.
We each wished to be 30 years younger,
livelier and healthier and stronger.
You'd think 30 would be enough, but no —
I'd take another 20 off, or so.
But thinking of the mess I made at 20,
I must concede, that old man's youth is plenty,
if 30 years suffice to clean it up —
which my fiancée demands in our prenup.

Spinoza's Birds (May 25, 2018, 5:30 AM–June 7, 2018)

It has bothered me for a long time that little if anything has been written about the psychological motives behind Baruch Spinoza's estrangement from the Community of Jews. A sufficient cause presented itself to my mind many years ago when I read a biography of the unfortunate Uriel Acosta. Acosta (ca 1585 - 1640), a presumed Marrano who converted back to Judaism only to slide into the heresies of Sadducism and atheism, was torn between a strong sense of Jewish identity and an overpowering need for rational insight into the complexities of Torah and Halachah. His repeated attempts to attach himself to the Community of Amsterdam while arguing with his rabbis and teachers eventually brought him to public disgrace and ultimately suicide. The biographer (a number of biographies have been written, and I do not remember which one I read), noted that the young Baruch, whose brilliance had already marked him for the Rabbinate, was almost certainly among the Congregants who symbolically trampled the prostrate body of Acosta on Yom Kippur, in or around the year 1640. The impression left by this horrifying spectacle upon the mind of an eight-year-old child cannot be ignored in evaluating the grown man's philosophical legacy.
    Notes to the poem are at the end.

If Spinoza's God were a Bird
would it be a bird of paradise?
The apotheosis would entail
a clarification: plant or animal? [1]
I was thinking of a choice of bird —
or more accurately, a bird of choice,
a manucode, a peacock
a strutting iridescence,
an *arfak astrapia* upside down
reflecting purple, green or bronze
depending on the angle of the light.

Or a lyrebird, less ocularly lavish, perhaps,
but intoxicating, orally, to the ear —
so much so, that a blind bard
would think himself before
a deity of sound
spilling epiphanies
to Trebizond
or oracles to tweeters.

He wouldn't pray to it
for that would be taking the bird's name in vain
but would admire it, overawed
and love it intellectually as God.

What is this God, then, so gloriously vague,
of the saintly hermit of The Hague?
Is this Divinity capricious, or just vivacious
like the Venus of the poet Lucretius? [2]
Is it a bird that does a mating dance
without a mate, without desire or love or lust,
a wind-up bird wound up by a wind-up toy —
a very wound-up, wounded little boy?

The 39 species of Birds
of Paradise, spectacular in thirds
for plumage, choreography and song,
remind me, other things among,
of that tender witness to a great wrong —
the 39 stripes administered
to a repentant Zadokite rum bird,
and his humiliation on Atonement Day
upon the threshold of the *esnoge*
as worshippers stepped over him to pray.

And ever since, as would have you or I,
he nurtured an irrepressible contempt
for costume and propriety
masquerading as faith and piety,
and struggled to conceive a God
Who'd countenance the laying of such a rod
upon the back of a sick and broken man.

It is, perhaps, a rather curious thing:
the story has such a familiar ring —
because nearly the converse fell to me
when I was just about as young as he.
My *imma* told me of Yemeni Jews
rescued by Israel, before it hit the news.
Imma proudly repeated what she'd heard
from a high-ranking diplomatic bird
and in my innocence I remonstrated,
"But is it right, just 'cause they're antiquated,
to cut their beards and *peyes* if they don't want?"
And *Imma* dropped her jaw and, repentant,
phoned up that bird and shared what I had said.
And thus came I to Torah; thus you fled!

Esteemed Philosopher, *Rachmana Litzlan*!
your sin was, you were smarter than
your teachers, but not as smart as the *Rambam*.
Her own *tzaraas* banned you from Amsterdam!
How long before the Edict is repealed?
You are the bird set free upon the open field! [3]

1. *Strelitzia*, commonly known as Bird of Paradise, is a plant native to South Africa yet emblematic of Southern California.

2. The Lucretian Venus has nothing to do with paganism. She is simply a metaphor for Nature's law of reproduction, and, more generally, for the infinite productivity of nature in its creative aspect. That Spinoza had studied the Epicureans is known, but his particular admiration for the *De Rerum Natura* of the great Roman poet, Lucretius, is revealed in the sentence (*Tractatus Theologico-Politicus, Praefatio*, Para. 1), "*Tantum timor homines insanire facit*," which echoes the famous verse, "*Tantum potuit religio suadere malorum*," (*De Rerum Natura*, I, 101). Moreover, Spinoza's apparent identification of God with Nature ("*Deus sive natura*"), encompassing both the physical universe and its underlying laws, is clearly in harmony with, if not inspired by, the rapturously contemplative religion prescribed by Lucretius as the surest pathway to a serene life.

3. Lev. 14: 4-7.

Protest (June 21, 2018)

A friend of mine, a son of Jewish father,
when asked, would he convert, replied, "No, never!"
And yet, this friend longed for a Jewish *kever*
beside his parents' graves — they lie together,

his mother having latterly converted,
leaving the son, if I might say, to fend
for himself. But it's no easier to blend
in with the living than the dead. I heard it

said, or read it, that the immortal soul
of such a child is Jewish, though interred
in Goyish body. A wanderer without rest,

a Jew among Gentiles, a Goy in Shul!
I asked my friend, "Why, then, won't you convert?"
"I can't!" he answered. *"This is my protest!"*

A Parable (July 9, 2018)

A *Yid* saw a certain *maydele* and wanted to marry her. He went to her *shadchan* and presented his proposal. The *shadchan*, without forwarding the young man's proposal to the *maydele* (for she had given him her specifications), said no. The *Yid* went to a Holy Rebbe and asked for a *Brochah* to marry this girl. The Rebbe said no: "It is her decision. I cannot decide for her. She is the one who must decide." The *Yid* was devastated. He *davened* to Hashem, fasting and weeping bitter tears. Hashem was moved. By Providence, the girl found out about the proposal, made her inquiries, forgot her own prerequisites, and accepted. The marriage was not good, and both suffered together many years.

It is taught: Be careful what you *daven* for, lest Hashem grant your wish. However, you may ask, why was the *kalah* (bride) punished with years of suffering? After all, it was Hashem who softened her heart. What did she do to deserve this? The answer may be that she delegated an essential part of her power to decide (the prerogative to decline a proposal) to her representative.

The pain of being rejected by someone is exceeded only by the pain of rejecting. There is no honest way to avoid this pain. Perhaps it is the price one must pay for a happy marriage.

Windsock (July 8-31, 2018)

See how the wind slips on a sock,
pads quietly around the block —
so quietly, the wind must knock
before it opens wide the door.

See how the wind pulls on a boot
kicks over trees, crown over root
breaks into houses, steals the loot
scatters the spoils to all the four.

See how the wind now dons a veil,
follows that sailboat down the aisle.
Note how the wind keeps changing tale
while the captain labors to keep score.

Indeed, we often hear him say,
"Which way blows the wind today?"
"Is there a wind at all, or nay?"
"When will the wind take me ashore?"

Akila's Howl (July 29-31, 2018)

When Akila howls it isn't really
fire engines, ambulances, or the police.
Imprinted on his brain, a categorical imperative:
"Everybody now!" He sings a clear sweet alto
composing as he goes
a melody that could be poetry or prose.
Visions accompany his song — his fused with mine.
fir trees under snow, blazing full, the moon,
half full, a drunken whiskey bottle
on a shaky table. Opposite, a broken chair
makes small talk while I play solitaire.
The chimney moans over a hissing hearth,
while outside, the wind rehearses with the wolves.
Akila is my neighbor's dog. Sometimes I speak to him
through the wooden slats of fence.

He barks back at me and growls —
harmlessly, just to prove that he's on guard.
Most of the time he just putters in his yard.
Or sleeps. At this very moment, however,
he is camping in the Sequoias.
Which is why I'm thinking of him now.
What does he feel when he hears the real thing?
Does his heart lift up and shout, "Awake and sing!"?
What goes through his head when, licking the air
outside the window of his pickup truck
he sees a prowlcar go by, lights flashing, sirens ablare?
That poor dog is way too much alone.
Sometimes I get up on a box and throw him a stick.
He walks up to it, gives it a sniff, lies down again.
The pity is, he might be marked for greatness.
At least he won't end up stuffed like Balto
in some musty old museum.
When he comes home on Sunday night
he'll soon get back to crooning his old *Te Deum*
for accidents and traffic stops and fires.
Aside from the occasional outdoors event
his, like mine, is a life of the imagination.
What did I do with my old pup tent?

My Russian Novel (August 7 - 29, 2018)

I imagine myself as many people.
It doesn't take that much imagination.
I stuff them into a Russian novel.
Maybe some animals, too, why not?
A sheep, a goat, a dog, a couple cats.
Spiders too. Aren't they awesome?
They will do the weaving.
Nothing too far out, you know.
Not too complicated.
I don't want to get all tangled up in plots.

    Each one of my characters has his own distinct perspective.
Zek Zekevich, for example. He is asleep right now
So let's not talk about him just yet.
We don't want to wake him.
In fact, I'm tempted to wave away the fly
that's crawling on his vacant brow
like a Sunday stroll in Gorky Park.
So enough of Zek for the time being —
D'you hear? He's snoring, now, poor bastard,
catching Z's like fish, and throwing them back.
Come, let's move on. Let him sleep.
We'll fetch him later. Let him rest.
We want to find him at his best.
    Did you notice how I've added a housefly to the mix?
So now our cast of characters contains a spider *and* a fly!
I did it for the drama, for the pathos.
For the guilt. You see, this very morning
I boxed the ears of a certain fly who had expressed
an interest in my buttered toast and jam
only to discover him late this afternoon
rolled up like the *Evening Pravda* in a spiderweb.
"Help me, help me!" cried the fly.
The buzz that only hours before drove me insane
now moved me to profound compassion.
(Make a note of that and try to explain!)
    Natasha heard it too as she breezed by
but didn't stop. She recoils at violence —
and also, let us speak freely, at mawkish sentiment.
Besides, she's on her way to meet Sergei
at a small but overcrowded Paris café.
"Are you Sergei?" she inquires,
recognizing him by his navyblue beret.
"Have you ever seen a photo of a fly," she asks,
"seen through the eye of an electron microscope?
I have, and it isn't pretty! The conception of
a monstrous mind — ingenious but disturbed.
It is hard," she prods, "to understand
why a God would tell it to bear fruit and multiply!"

The fly Tasha is speaking of is not the one
met previously on the forehead of our snoozing friend,
nor the other one, poor fellow, now a jelly
percolating inside Praskovia's belly.
No. It's of an altogether different species.
   "For one thing," replies Sergei with a gallant smile,
"so a pretty geneticist might study her mutations!"
   Natasha and Sergei are just getting acquainted.
They met on *izvinite dot com*, a site for dating
which gave their compatibility a "Sputnik" rating.
Indeed, she earns her living through a microscope
while he squints through a telescope for his.
(Her pay is small, and his, perennially far away.)
Nevertheless, they don't see eye to eye.
He spends his nights scanning the sky,
waiting patiently for light from eons away.
She waits for changes in the fruit fly's genes
and doesn't know what patience means.
He finds her attractive, and wouldn't mind.
She sees him as a kind of dancing bear
pierced through the nose with an iron ring.
She'd gladly give his chain a tug or two.
Unfortunately, their fantasies are brought up short
when she lets fall she has a spare degree,
the second being a Masters in psychology.
This news, for Sergei, raises a red flag.
Their conversation begins to lag.
   Next day, Natasha phones him up to say
she needs a more decisive, more aggressive man,
or (to call it like the cat) an alpha concubine
who knows how to butt into the bread line.
   Sergei draws a deep sigh of relief.
He's seen the light and it didn't take a million years!
In fact, that night, he'd dreamed a hulking lens
hung over him, his brain and reproductive parts
all neatly sliced and panelled, Tasha taking notes
surrounded by admirers in white coats.

    Back at the Kremlin, breakfasting in bed
on Veuve Clicquot and caviar,
Natasha wonders if fruit flies exist
on other planets, then cuts her wrist
while Count Yaroslavsky (born in '47)
drones on how he fought at Stalingrad,
got a medal and went to heaven.

The Vicar (Aug. 21-29, 2018)

    When I say my prayers, my cats all gather round.
I don't know if it's just the sound
they like, the voice of their old friend,
or if in some strange way they understand.
They never studied Hebrew, the Holy Tongue,
but for all we know, each living thing
has memories of *Alef-Beis*, if, as the rabbis teach,
the world was made with Hebrew letters (*otiot*).
If I were, God forbid, bereft of speech,
I'd want to hang around the talkers and the sayers.
I'd skip the gossip, though, and gravitate to prayers.
So when my cats come round, I pay attention
to what I'm saying, and pray more as I ought —
with *kavanah* — concentration and intention.
    The rabbis say it is the signpost of a fool
to look devout when a goat walks into shul.
But if a goat approached me while I'm praying
I'd think it's just his way of saying
"Put in a good word for me, too!" — unless, surprise!
my prayer gets answered with a butt in the assize.
However, as long as there's no goat behind me,
my pious pussycats remind me
that if I pray God hear my cry,
so, at the very least, should I!

The Cloud (September 3, 2018)

There is a cloud outside my window.
It is gaining rapidly in size —
growing right before my eyes.
Now it is getting smaller, though.
Bigger. Smaller. Like something inside breathing
or a heart slowly beating
beating slowly in the sky
a big heart in the sky like a cloud
a cloudy heart beating almost aloud.
Whose heart is that? I ask.
What is breathing up there in the sky?
Something watching with a big blue eye.
What do you see, O big blue eye?
Do you see flowers gaily smiling?
Do you see trees reverently swaying?
Do you see sheep in safety grazing?
Do you see man, blue eye?
What is he doing, this man of yours?
Scheming cheating robbing stealing?
Meditating murder to seize power,
power at any cost, by any act or lie?
Then to what race do *I* belong? Give me a name!
The same, answers the big blue eye,
the same.

A Bagel's Lament (Sept. 22-Oct. 14, 2018, Feb. 24-25, 2020)

So I'm parked outside Velvel the Bagelmaker,
an old graybeard in a brown Studebaker
left hand stuck out the window like an idiot
holding a bagel, yesterday's old *Yediot
Achronot* unread, thrown on the mat.
My car's a wreck, one tire's a little flat.
I'm feeling pangs. It's time to end the fast.
No sooner said, a cyclist whizzes past

and deftly grabs the bagel from my hand
as smooth as silk, like it had all been planned.
    And suddenly, it struck me from left field
that there's neither force nor field in nature —
supramolecularly speaking, of course —
that's capable of forming a ringlike structure
without a central mass; and yet that ring
held none. The hoop rotated, as it were,
zero *ibn* zero, *ayin me'ayin*,*
around empty space; and still this space
declaimed, as eloquently as the mouth
of a Disraeli or Demosthenes,
the steps by which the bagel came to be
from furrowed field to kettle to baker's oast
bespeaking the rough hand and furrowed brow
of human demiurge, not holy ghost.
    And then I saw the circle of my life —
not as a bagel — but, let us say, a toroid
describing wheels around a central void.
This void, however, wouldn't speak! No word
could I elicit from its hungry maw
to explain the pesky inconsistencies
that spoil the elegance of the equation —
if there's a formula for *frum* and free.*
    Yet all the while it kept on governing
in silence the orbit that was me. *Is* me —
as if exhorting me to mold the clay,
to geometrize the toroid to a torus,
transform the timeline into testament.
    What is this mute, tempestuous vacancy,
this dour baker's *chi* that punches dough
into a doughnut interrogative,
a noose around the neck of my existence,
and bids me sing in ecstasy or swing?

        **See Notes at end of poem, next page.*

    The Rabbis say, "Learn Torah! *Mitzvos* do!"
"Fear God!" says Solomon Ecclesiastes.
"Busy yourself," advises common sense,
"with what distracts you from obsessive thoughts;
for idle fancies lead to keen regrets!"
    So there I was, contemplating the genius
of zero, meditating on the *p'nimius*
and the contours of my empty hand,
when suddenly, as from a distant land,
a voice intruded: "Sir?" I turned my head.
"Sir, you forgot your lox-and-creamcheese spread!"

    Notes: *zero ibn zero, ayin me'ayin*: Zero, son of zero; nothing from nothing.
           Frum: Observant of Jewish Law.
           P'nimius: The essential meaning.

Snapshot (November 5 - 9, 2018)

Some years ago, a friend of mine and I
drove up to Idyllwild in early fall,
hiked up the mountain backpacks and all,
we loath to halt till eventide drew nigh.

It was pitch dark by the time we pitched our tent.
We lit a fire, we ate, we talked, we slept.
But I awoke to the roar of pines windswept
by ocean tides, rolling and irruent,

and was reminded of a sea-surmounting
prospect as far and memorable as now
that night, when like a droned Upanishad

I listened wakeful to the ceaseless pounding
of breakers row after row after row
and thought quite frankly that I would go mad.

A few weeks later, my friend sent me a snapshot
of me, backpack and all, my face enraptured!

Laughing Buddha (December 11, 2018 – February 21, 2019)

The fog lay flat on the dark earth
oppressive and inert;
like a brooding mist over a bog
lay the inert, oppressive fog
like a Rothko painting
or like a lover fainting
between the spread thighs of the hills
between the round breasts of the hills
like an Indian summer on a sweaty plain
like a tule fog on my dull brain
as it tries to wrestle a living knot
of unleavened feelings into a halfbaked thought.

   When I lie down on my bed at night,
my left brain jumps aboard the right
poised pre-emptively for suicide
but when I turn on my other side
I sense a subtle, a weightless shift
as if the right hemisphere were cut adrift
a rowboat on a rising tide
laden with bromide and cantharide
oarless, rudderless, a tattered sail —
on my knees I kneel and bail and bail.

   'Tis but a dream, the owl said to the pussycat.
The cat replied, Imagine that!
Then let us paint our galleon pea-green
that we may sail the Spanish Main unseen!
So long, I said, as we don't start to think
lest notwithstanding everything we sink.
Then we must learn to swim, said puss to owl
Go on, you first. I'll hold the towel.

Miss Lona Ginsburg in her slippers
between the Big and Little Dippers
drifts down the stairs smooth as a breeze
and seated at the piano, tries the keys
then wakes the house with a Chopin Ballade –
flawless, according to her mom and dad.
Her practice done, the girl glides up the stairs
oblivious of the astounded stares,
remembering nothing, to her great chagrin
on wakening of how she aced Chopin.

   But let's stop beating round the Mezibuzh:
Two roads divided in the bush
both trodden by the selfsame man
legs arched over a gaping span
as he pursues two paths astride
a yawning gulf toward a great divide.
Despite the abyss, can he – not fall –
but grow proportionately broad and tall –
a cedar rooted high and low
connecting cliffs and plains below?

   How long can a man divided stand
before he sinks into the sand?
Before his height and girth
swallow the entire earth?
Then what shall be his place
a homeless wanderer alone in space?
Unless the earth could reabsorb
that primal mist into its orb
and Rothko's rectangles overlap
and melt into an elevation map
the man peer through a peridot
to forge a novel kind of thought
that merges two paths into one
or two black oblongs into a sun
like a savant's number synesthesis –
pictograms for aposiopesis.

For instance, take an organ fugue by Bach.
You listen rapt, attentively, then, "*Ach!*"
you say, "How inexpressibly Divine!"
meaning how every phrase falls into line
as if established there by natural law,
as if Bach only painted what he saw,
as if he only found it where, sublime
it had been glittering since the birth of time.
If only a man's life could be like that
and one could get another chance at bat!

Yet Bach might say, *Also einfach war es nicht!*
Es bedurfte Arbeit, Einblick, Uebersicht!
As hard to carry out as hard to find
strewn among counterfeits of every kind.

   The world's more like a prelude than a fugue.
Or perhaps more like a centrifuge —
certainly a refining process
with few gains and many losses
a filtering of a person culled
from the mix, the filtrate pulled
away from center — against its inborn will.
How yield and yet be faithful still
how not betray, not compromise
yet in the end retrieve the prize
as in a classic novelette
tout pure au fond de l'éprouvette?

   Hard to grope one's way through life
and not stick someone with a pocket knife.
We have a wound, we have the stain to prove it.
The question is, how heal it? How remove it?
And where are we to find the smithy
who'll beat your blade into a trowel, I prithee?
Ecce Ockham's Blade of the Unconscious —
descried through Jung's insights and fearful hunches —
the psychic chancellor of the exchequer,
distiller of the treacherous liquor

of the passions — love, hate, blind exaltation —
that lead men drunk to the brink of annihilation,
lord keeper of the unwieldy key
to the imprisoned personality,
the Siloam of insight and intuition,
the firewood of courage and the ignition,
proclaimed by Freud to the antipodes,
the Oy-oy of despair of Oidipodes
the blinding flash that precedes
the *Heureka* of Archimedes,
the archetype of Orpheus in Hades
(the song awakening the soul that fades?)
the tears and smiles with which is laden
Schubert's music — aye, *Death and the Maiden!*
In sum, the cord that binds man's soul to God,
the sole of that man's foot to clay and clod.

   There is a waltz of what the Greeks called Fate
with some instinct, congenital, innate,
to sense which way the wind is blowing,
change course before the actual knowing.
And those who know "in advance of" —
the Rebbe my Rebbe or the Baal Shem Tov.
For beneath both kinds of thought
lurks this other thing God wrought
that none may fathom yet all may feel —
like being brushed by an electric eel
while diving in the briny deep.
You wake up suddenly from years of sleep
and, sprouting from no prior thought
like rain after a lengthy drought,
something comes into your head
and you advance, advised you should have fled
and lo, you've made an empire of Greece
built on a Grand Idea or a caprice;
or you've composed a Bach Cantata
or perhaps a Beethoven Sonata

and stand amazed, bemused, abashed in wonder
as the very heavens split asunder
or shower colorshapes on you futharking
numbers like the Prodigy of Barking,
or wafting wavicles through perforations
on paths determined by your observations.

   In Bengal, once, they built a high berm road
through wetlands. After the Flood
of 'Forty-two, a small river flowed
where they had built the road.
Inspecting the disastrous aftermath
of the cyclone's unforgiving path
and faced with a chorus of shamefaced regret
for so much wasted work and sweat
Binay Sen, India's CEO of Food
wanting to lift the general mood
is said to have consoled the local head,
"Better you had dug a ditch instead!"

   Our grave is dug the day we're born
yet when a loved one dies we mourn
though it be our turn the day after.
Can you not hear the Buddha's laughter?
How joy and sorrow alternate
though joined at the root in the substrate?
As deep we dig down through the layers
we're still stuck in the same state of affairs —
immersed head-first into the vortex
between medulla and prefrontal cortex.
Abi gezint, he laughs, with just a hint
of irony, *abi gezint!*
As long as you are healthy,
as long as you're a Jew!
As long as all the tears and smiles
were real — and not a crocodile's!

The Silent Teapot (March 1-2, 2019)

This morning I am sad
The teacup didn't talk.
See, when I brew my tea
I put aside the lid
turn down the cup
and set it on the pot
to keep it hot
and let it steep.
They make a perfect fit
the cup and pot
so when the heat comes up
it warms the cup.
The rising steam
makes the china clink
ching ching.
Such a small thing!

The Pyromane: on Rereading a Poem by Robert Frost (April 2019)

You'd think that now the fire's grown meek and cool
and mellowed to a comfortable glow
I'd be content to let the flame burn low
and not stoke the embers like a bloody fool,

or poke through the underbrush looking for fuel
to set these lovely woods ablaze; but no —
even though, whose woods these are, I think I know,
and there's a siren in his woodsy pool —

a glimmer of reflection and renewal.
He too hears voices singing sweet and low;
he still has far, I've not so far to go;
he has a horse; I have a stubborn mule.

But here's where I part ways with Mr. Frost:
These woods are mine, and I'm completely lost!

The Safety Pin (April 27-May 14, 2019)

The patch of moisture brings me round full circle.
When I was two or thereabout, my mother
scolded me, soft and solicitous:
"You have a potty now. You're not a baby
any more. Why do you keep on wetting
in your diaper?" To which, she said, I answered:
"But Mommy, if you want me to go potty,
why do you keep putting me in diapers?"
Or words to that effect and circumstance.
    My mother took the hint and ever since
I've managed myself more or less alright.
    I had no memory of this myself.
The story had faded with the morning news
that makes a myth of one's own late edition.
My mother told it me, still sitting proud
of my precocity, or as if to ask
in her discreet, sweet, motherly way of asking,
wasn't it high time that I got off the pot?
    But this she had forgotten, and her recounting
jogged the package off the memory train:
When I was all of mewling six months old
laid on my back upon the changing table,
a sharp pain pricked the left cheek of my bottom.
I cried. Distraught, my mother pleaded
"What is it? What's the matter?" Over and over.
Well, I wanted to explain, but didn't talk
so couldn't say; and not knowing how to speak,
the pain I felt was just as sharp a pain
as an open safety pin piercing my flesh.
    And that's precisely what I'm feeling now —
and I can't even remember how to cry!

Janus or Sejanus (May 16-29, 2019, February 2-23, 2020)

La Cordanata – the magnificent steps that descend from the Piazza del Campidoglio – lead away from the ancient Forum, not towards it, as I falsely remembered at a distance of more than 40 years. In antiquity, the stairway to the Forum led down from the other side of the Capitoline, affording the populace below a clear view of executed traitors (foremost among whom Sejanus, the mastermind of an infamous palace coup) thrown there for carrion and the vengeance of outraged citizens.

I remember walking down
a sweep of steps —
was it the Cordonata? —
holding back the tears.
An eerie hush, an August heat
hung o'er the *scalinata*,
o'er the City and its thoroughfares.
The Roman Forum at my feet,
unscrolled and brailled
like a blind man's manuscript!
Then

BOOM!

From the Gianiculo
a canon fired Noon.
The concussion rolled and whipped
from hill to hill
rebounding off two thousand years
through which, it seemed, I'd slept.
It travelled up and down my spine
from toe to crown.
I felt a chill and all but wept.

Except today
it's not that way.
Facing the Pantheon
I would be standing
back to the Forum
its squares and wares,
the Senate poised above,
the People at my heels.
It must have been
the Gemonian Stairs
I was thinking of.

Book Case (May 29-30, 2019)

"What kind of man," she asked, or rather said,
her tongue a cutting tool, her voice an awl,
"sleeps with a fucking library in his bed!"
as I drew back the covers and bed spread,
revealing volume three of *The Decline and Fall*.
Deeply offended, she did up her ribbon
and left me to enjoy the night with Gibbon.

Androcles (June 3, 2019)

This morning I saw a lion on the sky
much like a kittycat on a glass table
his paws stretched out in the familiar pose.
A pretty cloud, but I sensed something wrong —
how he stuck out his formidable paw,
and all the fierceness in his eye was gone.
Then I imagined I could hear him moan
and looking closer, thought I saw a thorn
deeply imbedded in the swollen pad.
On impulse I reached up to pull it out
but found that I could not reach high enough.
After all, the lion lay upon the sky
and I with all my good intentions lay
bound hand and foot and muzzled on the ground.

The Painted Lady (June 11, 2019)

The foothills blush with a bloom of painted ladies!
For weeks their ochre hordes had flown
right through my yard, through the entire town
to choruses of awe and accolades.

Spectator to the pageant of yellow and brown,
I'd mused, which member of those cavalcades
would, signaling an end to the parades,
bring up the rear with pennant of renown?

A loaded question from a troubled heart!
Today I got my answer. I should have known:
A single specimen still clad bright yellow

skirted the grass, aimless, alone, apart.
I offered him my finger, bending down,
which he avoided, not kenning a fellow.

A Tale of Two Cities (June 17–30, 2019)

By this irreverent tribute to a great philosopher and man of extraordinary courage, I mean only to draw attention to a pitfall shared by virtually all utopian thinkers if not all political philosophers. In my mind, the portrait of Campanella hangs next to Beethoven's as a memento perseverare. Moreover, it is arguable from the structure of Campanella's City ("Taprobano", presumably derived from Taprobana, an ancient name for the Island of Sri Lanka) that he conceived it as an allegory of the human psyche rather than as a serious venture into statecraft. However that may be, I find it opportune to add here an incident from Campanella's life that is generally omitted from modern histories of philosophy. The translation is my own:

> "Carlo Caffa, in a letter addressed to G.A. Schmidt reproduced in Cipriano's biography of Campanella, claims to have learned from an old Domenican Padre, a fellow student of our philosopher (TC) that he 'was in his youth, among all his classmates and fellow novices, of so undeveloped intellect that he was held in contempt and ridicule. How is that possible?! It happened one day that entering by chance into the cloisters [of the Convento di San Giorgio], he made the acquaintance of a certain wayfarer who was also walking there. The latter, taking him to a little apartment (*studiolo*) dwelt with him continuously for eight days, far from his regimen [*le discipline*] and his companions. After this time, [Campanella] appeared a changed man in respect of his intellectual ability, and from thenceforth, they found him in all his exercises and in the application of his studies different from what he had been before.['] This, the said octogenarian Padre and fellow student told me of Campanella, adding that the said wayfarer was ['] a Rabbi, who with the aid of a certain Kabbala, by a few brief principles endowed Campanella with such light that he arose in a short time such a great and admirable man.'"

The above passage is from a work entitled, *Sulla Vita e le Dottrine dell'Autore*, in *Opere di Tommaso Campanella, Scelte, Ordinate, ed Annotate da Alessandro d'Ancona* [author], *precedute da un discorso del medesimo*, pp. XIV-XV. Torino: Cugini Piombo e Comp. (1854). It is cited to "Cons. Echard et Quétif, Scriptores Domenic." [Scriptores ordinis praedicatorum recensiti, notisque historicis et criticis illustrati], by Quétif, Jacques, 1618-1698; Échard, Jacques, 1644-1724.

The story is corroborated by the following passage from the Campanella Archives: Archivio dei Filosofi del Rinascimento / Archivio Tommaso Campanella, http://www.iliesi.cnr.it/ATC/crono1.php?id=A1594_2&se=1:

"Al principio dell'anno [1594, TC] viene arrestato a Padova per ordine dell'Inquisizione, insieme con Giambattista Clario e Ottavio Longo. Subisce un terzo processo a seguito dell'accusa di aver disputato de fide con un giudaizzante senza averlo denunciato all'Inquisizione."

Translation:

"At the beginning of the year [1594, Campanella] is arrested at Padua by order of the Inquisition, together with Giambattista Clario and Ottavio Longo. He undergoes a third trial, standing accused of having held a disputation on the Faith with a practitioner of Judaism, without having reported him to the Inquisition."

[My thanks to Archive.org for the use of the excerpt from *Opere di Tommaso Campanella*; and to the Archivio dei Filosofi del Rinascimento for the excerpt from their chronology of the life of Campanella. – P.G.]

The City of the Sun and California City –
unlikely pair – have more in common than you'd think
despite being born a square 400 years apart.
Each founded on imaginary tracts of real
estate, one cost its visionary broker-preacher
his liberty and by a hair his tonsured head.
The younger speculator merely lost his pants
but died soon after in debt (the elder died in France).

Both men revered the sage for whom the sun stood still.
One named a hill for him, from which to cry, "Ye men
of Galilee, why gaze ye heavenward bedridden,
when lieth here before ye green acreage of Eden?"

The other wrote, when Galilei first went to trial,
a long amicus brief, still aching from the rack,
and penned *The City of the Sun* from a dark cell.
The latter's name, once infamous, still rings a bell;
the former's, all but forgotten. Just as well.

   What really binds the two of them is the pesky bug
that bit the ill-starred duo "where the sun *don't* shine!"
I mean Tom Campanella and Nat Mendelsohn,
distinguished realtors of the realty of the sun.
Utopia was the bug, myopia the illness;
for vision, seeing no further than the far horizon,
will tightly shut its eyes when it tips over the rim.
These men drew soldiers' maps, eyes riveted to the sky —
as if ours were but to follow and not reason why.

   Fortunate are you, Nat Mendelsohn! You dreamed
of turning arid desert into green and gold
and not of governing the customers you sold!
And doubly art thou fortunate, O Fra' Tommaso
in that you never built your mythic domicile —
prevented by decades of prison and exile.

   For every Taprobano rests upon the premise
that society is like a symphony
with every player playing in tune and harmony
to the tap-tap-tapping of a perfectly designed
adroitly balanced dainty philharmonic stick —
a rare enough phenomenon in a concert hall,
where we applaud if the utopia maintain
for ninety minutes (not counting twenty for champagne)!

   Hence all utopias conceal a sound-proof chamber,
every Shangri-La is built over a basement;
an offshore island cove conceals a labor camp,
the eighteenth golf-course hole, a crematorium —
all in the interest of an undisclosed agenda
to turn the People into "Prisoners of Zenda."

    A few miles east of Monolith, there stands a sign,
the only erect thing for miles of empty clay,
that hails the Vegas-bound vacationer hurtling past,
"Welcome to California City!"
                      Home at last!

Schubert's Fantasy (July 2, 2019)

Schubert's great C minor
Sonata D nine fifty-eight,
as printed on the jacket liner,
opens with the theme of Beethoven's
C minor Variations on a Theme.
If we examined this through untinted lens,
and did not know the actual date,
we might conclude (for it might seem)
that Beethoven composed variations on Schubert's theme!
And nothing could have given Schubert more delight
than such a major oversight!
Was this his fantasy, composing nine fifty-eight?
Or is it mine? Who else's might it have been?
Useless to speculate!
In the next universe over, if we could tear the screen,
Beethoven dreams Schubert made great music from his theme
and Schubert fantasizes in a dream
that someone wrote a poem about it (see this text).
From here we learn, from this we glean
there's not much variation between
one infinite universe and the next.

Visit (July 3, 2019)

They say that birds are chariots for souls
and visit us when we're about to die
and ferry us on feathered wings on high
or downward to a nest of fiery coals.

Sometimes, however, 'tis said, they will switch roles
and souls will requisition birds to fly
them to their loved ones when they hear them cry
like glider pilots glued to the controls.

Just yesterday a pair of sparrows lighted
upon a chair outside my open door
and chirped and chastised me *di tutto cuor*.
And I chirped back, as though to say, "Delighted!"

But then, one moved aside, and then the other,
flying through the open door, made straight for me!
As Dante writes in his great Comedy,
"*Quali colombe*," so hastened the mother

to her child, now old and bent and white.
And fearing for her safety, I quickly raised
my hands. "No, no!" I said, standing amazed
as she re-joined her mate and both took flight.

I smiled to think myself in nest or nursery.
But through the smiles, I wiped away some tears
and sighed, "Still lovers after all these years!"
For indeed, it was their wedding anniversary!

Translation of a Dalì Painting (July 9-14, 2019)

The painting is "Mia moglie, nuda, guarda il suo corpo diventare gradini, tre vertebre di una colonna, cielo e architettura". The artist's wife, seen from behind, "watches her body turn into stairs, three vertebrae of a column, sky and architecture."

I see you in my dreams, my darling wife,
éscalier au ciel de rêves et de cauchemars;
you are the architecture of my life,
my cervical, thoracic and lumbar,

my atlas and my axis columnar!
Palette in hand with brush and palette knife,
a dandelion beside a nilufar,
I annihilate myself in this still life;

while you, gazing into your bedroom mirror,
see nothing of the image that appears
nor the decapitated Grecian head

that smiles and weeps and drinks your form in terror —
not of the marble slab from which it peers
out of the Infinite Prohibited,

    but of the image in the voyeur's eyes
    and of the ecstasy concealed between her thighs.

At the Sign of the Swan: Five Translations & One Sonnet in a Whimcycle Setting (2019)

(Note: Stefan George's surname is pronounced "Ghe-órghe". His English, though competent, reveals his German nationality, whereas Mallarmé, who taught English for a living, is fluent in the language.)

I sat with Mallarmé and Stefan George,
the three of us at The Sign of the Swan.
Tennyson had sent word from the morgue
saying not to wait, he would be there anon.

We ordered ale for us, for Alf, a beer,
but bade the girl, a buxom, comely wench,
not draw it till the man himself appear.
Stefan German spoke, Stéphane spoke French.

Our topic was "*L'après-midi d'un faune*"
but drifted to a sonnet by Stéphane
that prophesied a brave, a bright new dawn
beclouded by the evening of a swan.

Stéphane, declining, conjured me to read it,
citing Lord Alfred's absence, and a cold.
My pleas of unpreparedness unheeded,
I opened to his poem and read it cold.

Le Vierge, le vivace

*Le vierge, le vivace et le bel aujourd'hui
Va-t-il nous déchirer avec un coup d'aile ivre
Ce lac dur oublié que hante sous le givre
Le transparent glacier des vols qui n'ont pas fui?*

*Un cygne d'autrefois se souvient que c'est lui
Magnifique mais qui sans espoir se délivre
Pour n'avoir pas chanté la région où vivre
Quand du stérile hiver a resplendi l'ennui.*

*Tout son col secouera cette blanche agonie
Par l'espace infligée à l'oiseau qui le nie,
Mais non l'horreur du sol où le plumage est pris.*

*Fantôme qu'à ce lieu son pur éclat assigne,
Il s'immobilise au songe froid de mépris
Que vêt parmi l'exil inutile le Cygne.*

For those of us who've not yet studied French,
I've made an English version I think better
than most — forgive my speaking from the bench —
that I have seen, in spirit and in letter:

The Sign of the Swan

This virginal and vital, beautiful new day —
will it smash for us with drunken stroke of wing
the hard, forgotten lake obsessed beneath the frost
by the glasslike glacier of flights not flown away?

A swan of other times remembers that it is he
who, though magnificent, gives himself up without a hope
for never having sung the landscape where one lives
when the ennui of sterile winter glitters bright.

With all his neck he'll shake off this white agony
through the very space decreed on space-negating birds,
but not the horror of the earth that tugs his plumage.

The very ghost that lends this place its pure explosiveness
he freezes in the cold dream of indifference
that the Swan wears amid its pointless exile.

Herr George bridled at this lovely sonnet
and made, I hazard, his objections known
in a dense poem. Not much is published on it
but here's the German; the English is my own:

Denk Nicht Zuviel (from Der Stern des Bundes, 1914, 1922)

Denk nicht zuviel von dem was keiner weiss!
Unhebbar ist der lebenbilder sinn:
Der wildschwan den du schossest den im hof
Du kurz noch hieltest mit zerbrochnem flügel
Er mahnte – sagtest du – an fernes wesen
Verwandtes dir das du in ihm vernichtet.
Er siechte ohne dank für deine pflege
Und ohne groll .. doch als sein ende kam
Schalt dich sein brechend auge dass du ihn
Um-triebst in einen neuen kreis der dinge.

A Wounded Swan

Think not too much about no one knows what!
You can't lift meaning from the living image.
The wild swan whom you shot and then brought home
with shattered wing to doctor up in court
reminded you (you said), of something vaguely
akin to you — which you destroyed in him.
He fades without a thank-you for your care,
without reproach, but still, when his end came
his parting eye cast a hard squint on you
for entangling him in a strange realm of things.

Stéphane took Stefan's poem as an attack
(I'm not quite sure his take was justified).
He stiffened in his chair, his jaw went slack;
he bit his tongue, then icily replied:

"The pot calling the kettle black, I think!
I know I threw a lot into my lake,
but you, you throw so much into your sink,
I hear the crash of dishes as they break!

You sit in state, exalt poetic purity
and yet you hide your poem behind a screen;
you clothe your words in veils of such obscurity
that no one has an inkling what they mean!"

"Who sees the whiteness of your swan in snow?"
retorted Stefan. Mallarmé replied,
"That's why you shot it? So the blood would show?
You say I tried to nurse it, but it died?"

"'*Sie war's*, not I, who shot!" rejoined Herr George.
"A martyr for a bright *Nouvelle Époque!*"
parried the Frenchman; "*Mach dir keine Sorgen!*" *
"*Prosit!*" said I. And then we drank our bock.

Now enter Tennyson, Baudelaire in tow.
"*J'unie un coeur de neige à la blancheur des cygnes,*" **
the Frenchman said, his wings drooping with snow.
"*Le sang de poète ne fait jamais de signes!*"

"*Stimmt,*" said George. "*Das meinte ich aber nicht.*
Who understands the *Todeskampf*, the pain,
the price a poet pays *für ein* Gedicht?
But *Klarheit* counts, lest poets write in vain!

  * Mach dir keine Sorgen: "Don't worry about it!"

  ** "I combine a heart of snow with the whiteness of swans." Baudelaire, Les Fleurs du Mal, "La beauté," v. 6. He continues, "The blood of poets never leaves a sign." George replies, "True, but that's not what I meant." Todeskampf = "deadly struggle"; Gedicht = "<u>poem</u>"; Klarheit = "clarity".

Of beauty, meaning is the holy grail;
make dark the sense, the beauty grows a beak!"
Here Tennyson stood us a round of ale.
"Banish the beer! And bring bubble and squeak!"

At this, inspired to follow Alfred's lead,
I intervened between the dueling strummers —
teacher and pupil — and asked Stefan to read
a passage I hold dear from "*Sieg des Sommers*,"

in which the poet recalls how as a child
(for I believe 'twas of himself he wrote)
he took the gift of poetry in the wild
from Thalia enswanned, her very throat!

From "*Sieg des sommers*" (Stefan George, *Das Jahr der Seele*, 1897)

Gemahnt dich noch das schöne bildnis dessen
Der nach den schluchten-rosen kühn gehascht ·
Der über seiner jagd den tag vergessen ·
Der von der dolden vollem seim genascht?

Der nach dem parke sich zur ruhe wandte ·
Trieb ihn ein flügelschillern allzuweit ·
Der sinnend sass an jenes weihers kante
Und lauschte in die tiefe heimlichkeit . . .

Und von der insel moosgekrönter steine
Verliess der schwan das spiel des wasserfalls
Und legte in die kinderhand die feine
Die schmeichelnde den schlanken hals.

When I speak *Deutsch*, I generally take a Luden's
but know enough to read and translate verse
with the assistance of my dog-eared Duden's
So here is my translation (could be worse):

Victory of Summer

Do you still hold the memory sublime
of him who, chasing roses of the glen,
in the ardor of the hunt lost track of time
and sucked the honey from the hips, and then

turned t'ward the gardens and a restful hedge –
and drawn to an all-too-distant flash of wings
sat by yon little pond at water's edge
and listened to the deepest, secret things;

and from its moss-grown stony islet strand
a swan the play of waterfalls forsook
and pushed into the child's extended hand,
gentle and caressing, its slender neck?

"*C'est beau!*" exclaimed the Frenchman, much appeased.
"How smooth your words, how sweet the music flows;
how effortlessly you massaged and squeezed
the essence and the sense from your wild rose!

I tried to teach a new poetic idiom
of homophones and non-hermetic symbolism.
I'd hoped you'd be a member of our presidium,
but you left us for an hermetic Germanism.

I remember when you came to me. How gifted
is the lad, I thought! How very promising!
Why would you misconstrue my '*Sinn*' as lifted
from a swan you parse as dying and grimacing?"

Now George drew a sigh and ran his fingers
through his wavy, histrionic hair,
selected ringing words with a bellringer's
ear, and spoke with professorial air:

"Long has Poetry been linked with birds —
both by their song, like Hesiod's nightingale,
and by immortal Homer's 'wingèd words.'
Your '*Vierge*' sends poetry beyond the pale,

into a 'pointless exile' among the stars!
What right have you to so abuse my *Schwan*,
the muse and mentor of my tender years,
who gave me poetry for my nastaran?"

Then Mallarmé allowed a quiet smile
to play upon his lips before he spoke.
"The best of poems are all penned in exile.
My own success has been my harshest yoke!

And that is what my sonnet called '*Le vierge*'
was trying to say in terms perhaps obscure —
that great success exiles the demiurge
in every artist with its bourgeois lure.

The exile of the Muse was in the air
long ere I tried to remedy the loss
of meaning from the word. Monsieur Baudelaire
announced it in his poem, 'The Albatross.'

Charles, reveillez-vous! Faites-nous ce petit plaisir!
Voici le livre, voici le rime: lisez!
Votre beau poème à peine se laisse traduire!
Peut-être Pierre saura le faire anglais." *

L'albatros de Baudelaire

Souvent, pour s'amuser, les hommes d'équipage
Prennent des albatros, vastes oiseaux des mers,
Qui suivent, indolents compagnons de voyage,
Le navire glissant sur les gouffres amers.

À peine les ont-ils déposés sur les planches,
Que ces rois de l'azur, maladroits et honteux,
Laissent piteusement leurs grandes ailes blanches
Comme des avirons traîner à côté d'eux.

Ce voyageur ailé, comme il est gauche et veule!
Lui, naguère si beau, qu'il est comique et laid!
L'un agace son bec avec un brûle-gueule,
L'autre mime, en boitant, l'infirme qui volait!

Le Poète est semblable au prince des nuées
Qui hante la tempête et se rit de l'archer;
Exilé sur le sol au milieu des huées,
Ses ailes de géant l'empêchent de marcher.

* "Charles, wake up! Do us this small favor! Here is the book, here
is the poem: read! Your beautiful verses hardly allow for translation!
Maybe Peter will know how to make it English."

The Albatross (translation for Francesco Benedetti)

It happens that for fun the men of a ship's crew
will seize an albatross, birds of immense wingspan
that follow lazily, like fellow voyagers,
a vessel skimming bitter swells of océan.

As soon deposited upon the wooden deck,
those sovereigns of the blue, ungainly and mortified,
pathetically drag their white prodigious wings —
like pairs of rowing oars hung loosely at their side.

That wingèd argonaut, how clumsy now! How weak!
A while ago so handsome, now an ugly clown!
One of the men profanes with lit cheroot his beak.
Another, lurching, mocks a cripple who has flown!

The poet has much in common with the prince of clouds
that haunts the tempest and derides the hunter's stalking.
Exiled upon the earth mid howlings of the mob,
his giant poet wings prevent the man from walking.

Now German George, exact to the extreme,
complained, "*Ein Albatros ist nicht ein Schwan!*
What means this change of . . . poultry in midstream?!
Let us respect *den ursprünglichen Plan!*" *

"*Mais M'sieur, j'ai bien ecrit un beau poème
sur un cygnet!*" protested Charles Baudelaire.
"Indeed you have," I said, "and what a gem!
Récitez-nous, je vous en prie les vers . . .

* George: "An albatross is not a swan . . . . Let us respect the original plan!" Baudelaire: "But sir, I have written a beautiful poem about a swan!" Peter: "Please recite for us the lines that relate to our subject — (next page) with one qualification:"

qui touchent – avec une glose – à notre matière!
Because your swan stands for the tragic fate
of exiles, not the burden poets bear.
You read your French, and I'll try to translate."

"My friend, *vous vous trompez!*" intoned a voice*
from across the crowded room. It was Rimbaud!
"What image for a poet could be more choice
than a swan crying for a puddle unto God!"

From Baudelaire's *"Le cygne"*

Là s'étalait jadis une ménagerie;
Là je vis, un matin, à l'heure où sous les cieux
Froids et clairs le Travail s'éveille, où la voirie
Pousse un sombre ouragan dans l'air silencieux,

Un cygne qui s'était évadé de sa cage,
Et, de ses pieds palmés frottant le pavé sec,
Sur le sol raboteux traînait son blanc plumage.
Près d'un ruisseau sans eau la bête ouvrant le bec

Baignait nerveusement ses ailes dans la poudre,
Et disait, le coeur plein de son beau lac natal:
«Eau, quand donc pleuvras-tu? quand tonneras-tu, foudre?»
Je vois ce malheureux, mythe étrange et fatal,

Vers le ciel quelquefois, comme l'homme d'Ovide,
Vers le ciel ironique et cruellement bleu,
Sur son cou convulsif tendant sa tête avide
Comme s'il adressait des reproches à Dieu!

* Voice: "You are mistaken!"

If ever flowers bloomed from evil soil,
these verses of the famed *"Poète Maudit"*
assuage the ear — and set the blood to boil!
The words one might translate; *jamais l'esprit!*

A Captive Swan

Yonder, there used to stand a small menagerie.
One morning early, when beneath the cold, clear sky
the workers rouse, and Public Roads sweeps foul debris —
dust storms into the stillness — something caught my eye.

A swan who had contrived to escape his captive cage
beat a dry path with his web feet to an empty rill
trailing on the broken ground his white plumage,
and settling there, the poor beast, opening wide his bill

sprinkled his frantic wings with dirt in the parched gutter
and called, his heart filled with the lake where he was born,
"When will you thunder, lightning? When will you rain, water?"
I see this suffering creature, mythic, strange, forlorn

extending his convulsive neck, his thirsting head
sometimes up to the sky, like Ovid's First Man,* even
up to the savage sky, ironically blue-spread
as if crying out his grievance unto God in Heaven.

*P. Ovidius Naso, *Metamorphoses* I, vv. 84-86:

Pronaque cum spectent animalia cetera terram,
os homini sublime dedit, caelumque videre
iussit et erectos ad sidera tollere vultus.

Translation (1567) by Arthur Golding (1536 - 1606)

And where all other beasts behold the ground with groveling eie,
He gave to Man a stately looke replete with majestie.
And willde him to behold the Heaven wyth countnance cast on hie,

And so the albatross of Charles Baudelaire
was changed into a poet-swan again
and Stefan George inveigled to declare
duly restored the swan to her domain.

"Restored, perhaps," I said; "revivèd, no!
Though poetry be not dead, her spirit died
with *vierge, vivace et bel*, snuffed years ago
by Deconstruction and the TV Guide,

by the entropy of estrus and the atrophy,
by jokers wild, blank tiles, blank checks and squigs
by sexual politics and the catastrophe
of quotas, SATs and Myers-Briggs.

And by the plague of self-perpetuating
creative writing teachers and their courses —
like puppy mills and stud farms generating
inbred dogs and arteritic horses."

Now Tennyson read "Tithonus". We wept.
Then Mallarmé ahemmed as if to speak.
George yawned, Baudelaire smokedreamed or slept:
but I wrote down in my *cahier pratique*:

Mallarmé to Tennyson

"And after many a summer dies the swan." *
His beauty does not merit eternal life;
only a reflecting pool to reflect upon
that twins his image, or splits it like a knife —

the real from the unreal, yet unifying,
as if to signify that beauty borne
on mortal wing perishes not on dying
but reaffirms itself as though reborn.

   * Tennyson, "Tithonus," v. 4

"Thou wilt renew thy beauty morn by morn," *
laments, eternally growing old, Tithonus.
But more: the swan — my swan — can never die

though dead, nor can I find in me to mourn
the eternal sign with its eternal onus —
beneath the lake, another swan, and I.

* Tennyson, "Tithonus," v. 74.

A Brief Note on Mallarmé and George

In school we were taught that words are attached to meanings, and the attachment is preserved in dictionaries. The lesson serves well enough for mundane communication. The reality, as is well known to students of linguistic and literary theory, is more complicated. The relationship between words and meaning is fluid. It constantly changes, not merely through time, but through the countless associations—both conscious and unconscious, symbolic, metaphorical and personal—that consummate their ephemeral union as a creative or interpretive offering.

A similar process takes place in the reader—not as a reflection, but as a more or less distant echo. That is why I reject the idea that there can be an authoritative understanding of a poem. The beauty of a good poem is that it presents itself as a living cloud of plausible meanings, not as an encoded message that awaits a savant with a golden key. Like a cloud of interstellar dust, each poem-cloud does indeed contain a center of gravity around which the weightiest interpretations coalesce, but there remains a halo of personal significances that cannot be generalized. A tune that leaves me utterly cold brings tears to another man's eyes: "Honey, they are playing our song!" It goes without saying that somewhere in this poem-cloud floats the meaning *once* intended by the poet. But where? And years later, will the poet himself remember exactly what he was thinking of?

How essential is it to the life of a poem that the reader "catch" the precise meaning the poet intended? Bear in mind that if a poet has a clear, specific message that she wants to deliver, she will generally write it in expository prose. The lyric poem, like music, is not governed alone by an oligarchy of logical, rhetorical, grammatical and syntactical rules.

It is composed *ab initio* as a "cloud" of competing ideas, image-thoughts and emotions; and when theorists talk of "decoding" a poem, it is worth remembering that probably there was never an unambiguous "code" to begin with, and that, without the reader, with his sometimes silly or baseless interpretations, there is no poem at all.

In the case of Mallarmé or Stefan George, it is especially hard to arrive at a core of interpretive consensus, because each of these two poets strives, at the expense of conventional syntax, phraseology and lexicon, to fashion a mode of speech deliberately based on a halo of unarticulated or incompletely articulated associations, with the result that the core idea is blurred or obscured, albeit greatly enriched.

Obviously, the intent (at least in the case of Mallarmé) is, generally speaking, not to conceal the meaning, but to render it more mysterious and organically alive. Mallarmé uses superficially unrelated objects (that is to say: the words denoting those objects) to arouse thoughts and feelings through image and sound; but he uses those objects in the context of their familiar, usual function and appearance. He also uses homophones to add to the semantic weight of a chosen word.

Thus, reaching the core of Mallarmé's symbolist poems demands considerable creative effort, but not without reward. In *"Le vierge,"* the introduction of a swan evokes in me a visual/emotional impression comparable to what I feel when I look at a living swan. But the verb *se souvient* ("remembers") lifts the imagined swan from the natural world to that of human associations. Thus, "a swan of other times remembers" invites me to envision the author wistfully recalling how in times past he wrote poems swanlike in beauty and inspiration. It is left to the reader to construct analogous associations around the frost-covered, frozen surface of the lake, the imprisoned depths beneath, the strenuous launch into the air, the pull of gravity, the cold, white bleakness of the scene, and the final, contrasting allusion to the Swan Constellation, which exiles the swan-poet to a remote sphere, impotent, abstract, and removed from human emotion—yet not so removed that he does not feel horror at the prospect of failure or of mortality.

This formula is complicated by Mallarmé's introduction of the homophonic allusions, *cygne/signe* (swan/sign) and *coup d'aile ivre/coup de livre* (drunken stroke of wing / powerful impression left by a book), and possibly others. The *signe*, in its linguistic meaning, is obviously relevant to Mallarmé's symbolic use of the swan. But while the poet seems to imply that his outburst of inebriate enthusiasm was set off by something he read in a book, the poem does not tell us which book. Hence, knowing precisely which one can't be of great importance to an interpreter of the poem, though it might be to a biographer of the poet.

Nevertheless, I suspect that here there is indeed a "golden key" to this poem, known only to Mallarmé and his inner circle. For "*Le vierge, le vivace*" seems to celebrate the birth of a grand idea—the inspiration, perhaps still vague in the poet's mind, for a radically new kind of poem that will tear up (*déchirer*) the frozen poetic conventions of the past—a poem that will ultimately be completed and published (1897) as the poem-book, *Un coup de dés* (A roll of the dice)!

Short of express mention in the poet's correspondence or other papers, it is difficult to prove the exact moment when this great idea was born. "*Le vierge, le vivace*" first appeared in print in 1885. However, a letter of Mallarmé to Henri Cazalis (May 14, 1867), in which he confesses to harboring intense feelings of alienation, self-abstraction, and feigned indifference akin to those expressed in "*Le vierge*," suggests a much earlier date for the composition of that poem with its presentiment of a revolutionary "*coup de livre*." For now, let us add this tantalizing possibility to the cloud of meaning surrounding the poem.

But there is another cloud, closely related to the former, that must be dealt with. A youthful admirer of Mallarmé, Stefan George cultivated an early fascination with the French Symbolists. He attended, during a brief sojourn in Paris, the latter's famous Tuesday *Soirées*, submitting poems composed in French. At some point, for unknown reasons, there was a falling out, and George returned to Germany, never again to publish French verse. From his native German, he gradually developed a highly condensed syntax and a rather disjointed, idiosyncratic style. George's earlier poems, such as the excerpt I translated from "Victory of Summer," are characterized by a pastoral, Theocritan style, but they are already marked by an unmistakably allegorical symbolism. However, the poem I have translated as "A Wounded Swan" ("*Denk nicht zu viel*") is from *Der Stern des Bundes* (1914, 1922), a collection of George's later poems. These poems are heavily clad in allegorical metaphor, as in Mallarmé, but in *Der Stern*, the allegory serves a rhetorical rather than a visual function. Written primarily for his own followers, and sometimes *ad hominem*, they seem deliberately to conceal his meaning from extraneous persons.

The foregoing suggests an allusive intent behind George's poem, "*Denk nicht zuviel*," aiming at something written by another poet—perhaps (why not?) Mallarmé himself! Of course, Mallarmé had been dead for 16 years when "*Denk nicht zuviel*" first appeared, but George would not have wanted to broadcast to all and sundry the identity of the person so carefully camouflaged in it. Still, George must have felt a lingering resentment for his Paris treatment—real or imagined—by the Frenchman, whose fame, meanwhile, had exalted him to a hallowed place in the firmament of French literature. Moreover, George will have regarded "*Le vierge*" (first published in 1885) with special ambivalence for its treatment of the swan image so dear to George's personal mythology. On the one hand, as a boy first reading the French Symbolists, George will have associated the author of "*Le vierge*" with the swan-muse remembered in *Sieg des Sommers*; on the other, years later, he will have rejected Mallarmé's transformation of George's personal muse into a cold and lifeless abstraction.

Linking the two poems in this manner is proposed as a creative act on my part, in the spirit of Hermann Hesse's *Glasperlenspiel* and Lévi-Strauss's *bricolage*, not as literary criticism, which would require a great deal more research and more familiarity with French and German—not to mention Mallarmé's and George's writings—than I currently possess.

Here is my reading of George's poem, on which I constructed the imagined pub-room quarrel between George and Mallarmé:

> One cannot lift meaning from a living object (by transforming it into a lifeless symbol)—like your swan, for example—only to transplant it into a foreign context which renders it arcane. Why search for the meaning of your Swan Constellation? You once shot a real "swan"—a wild swan—with your harsh criticism, and, though you brought him soon afterward to the hall (*Hof*) where you hold court, and attempted to mollify him with patronizing words ("I see myself in you; we are not unlike each other . . ."), you proceeded to tear him to pieces by enumerating all the ways in which *we* were *not* alike! And so I broke (*brechend Auge*) with you, with neither gratitude nor blame. And yet, in the last analysis, I can't help viewing you analytically, coldly, for drawing me into a strange circle where I do not belong.

Let us revisit for a moment the excerpt from George's *Sieg des Sommers*. (1897), just as George may have revisited "*Le vierge*": George was 17 when "*Le vierge*" first appeared (1885). His meeting with Mallarmé is thought to have occurred around 1889. Did the young George identify Mallarmé with the swan-muse to whom he paid grateful tribute in his early verses? Was "*Denk nicht zu viel*", which George published in 1914 (by which time he had secured his own literary eminence) his repudiation of the debt?

I leave it to the specialists to appraise my hypothesis, but let us not altogether remove it from the halo of plausible meanings surrounding George's bitter little epigram.

Cycni Signi Finis

The Music Box (November 23-24, 2019)

This guy on Youtube built this Rube Goldberg machine—
with belts, levers, ball bearings, gears, drumsticks and spoons.
He winds it up and pulls a crank to make it go.
It plays computer-generated manic tunes
with marbles shooting onto plates of steel or wood
from the barrel of a kind of semiquaver gun.
It's rather clever, really, all components working
together. The notes are all pre-funneled into it
like a music box, which is what it is, basically.
He's everywhere at once, pushing this, jerking that.
But get it going, and bite me if it doesn't run
by itself! He can relax and enjoy his work. He grins.
He designed and built it, and lo, it is very good!
Except the music, which is, quite frankly, so-so.

Freedom and Flannel Trousers (October 23, 2019)

> ". . . the group that stood for 'freedom' and flannel trousers. . ."
> D.H. Lawrence, *Lady Chatterly's Lover*.

When I wear these pants, I flutter and look up.
I have other pants, but I flutter when I wear these.
Dangerous pants! If I could just remember
it's only the pants and watch where I am going!

Luciole (Lightning Bugs) (June 28, 2020) For Luciano Capuccelli.

"Scusate! Non vi ho visti!"
said the gentleman, raising the barrel
as we scrambled to our feet.
You had forgotten. It was the first day of the season.
Or maybe the last.
We had gone for a tranquil hike
through the woods behind your orchard patch -
a winding country trail cut through a rise.

He'd fired from an embankment
where he now stood frozen,
boots planted just above our heads.
Shocked by the blast, we'd hurled ourselves
headlong into the dirt. *"Per carità!*
Per poco non ci hai ammazzati –
you could have killed us!
Fa attenzione!" was all you said.
I don't remember what we spoke of after that —
not philosophy in any case!
We took the hint and turned around.
No more reports. He must have done the same.
It was full evening when we emerged
into the looming sanctuary of your house.
As we approached, a cloud of flashing fireflies
appeared from nowhere, enfolded us
escorted us in luminous procession
to your front porch.

Girasole (June 24-26, 2020) For Luciano and Anna Capuccelli

Do you remember, caro Luciano,
that time so long ago
you drove us to Marsciano,
down to the Néstore
sweetflowing and garrulous
to fish for chub
with a kind of net —
an inverted pyramid
you placed beneath a limpid cataract?
How quickly the net filled up
with wriggling fish!
They poured in like water!
More than enough to cook,
the rest to lay on ice —
if there were room
in your old fridge!

Remember? Driving to the creek
we passed a field of sunflowers —
a whole battalion of them
standing at attention!
I asked you to pull over
"Let's take a look," I said,
dissembling my reasons.
Dismounting from your Rosinante
we joined the ranks
arms rigid at our side
chins uptilted to the sun.
Then you marched out in front
and launched into a speech by Lenin
you had memorized,
your eloquence cut short
by a burst of laughter,
your finger pointing behind me
to where one recalcitrant
faced obstinately the other way —
a phenomenon we just had
to inspect up close
and make a record of.
Remember how I tried to turn
the enormous head around?
I still have the photo!

On our way home, passing
the same now dormant field
I asked you once again
to stop so I could look him up,
our rebel friend,
amid a sea of drooping heads.
But it was getting late, you said,
Let's not keep Anna waiting.

Do you know, *Compagno*,
how often I returned there after dark
to marvel at a sunflower
shining in the night?

Around the Corner (Sept. 15-16, 2020)

I'm five or six again, deny my bones.
My parents have parked by this secluded lake
and I am happily throwing pebble stones
into the water for the splash the pebbles make.

"Peter, let's go! We must be on our way!"
I whine and whimper like a hired mourner.
But my mother and my father say,
"There's always something wonderful around the corner!"

And on the road, we see a man astride
a horse. My dad says "Hi!", leans out his head,
"Where can I find a horse my son could ride?"
The man says, "Follow me. My ranch is just ahead."

But when it's time to thank the man and horse,
I wail and whine forlorn and then forlorner!
My parents scold, "No fuss and no remorse!
"There's always something wonderful around the corner."

And as we tool down Highway 101
we pass a pier, the harbor boat still moored.
My dad pulls over off the road; I run
straight to the waiting harbor boat and jump on board.

My folks catch up, we launch into the foam.
A splendid sun sets as we round the bay
And now my father says, "Time to go home!"
How can I mourn so fine and beautiful a day?

An old man, now, I tell myself, a foreigner
in a foreign land, lying wide awake,
"There's something wonderful around the corner."
Yet I still linger here, throwing stones into a lake.

Dialog of Abraham and Isaac on the Way to the Mountain of Moriah: a Meditation on the Binding of Isaac (Gen. 22, 1-19). (Sept. 12 — Nov. 11, 2020).

It is customary for a Jew to prepare himself for the Morning Prayer by meditating on the Biblical passage, Gen. 22, 1-19–one of the most enigmatic passages in the Torah. The passage is meant to exemplify the Commandment to "Love God your Lord with all your heart, with all your soul and with all your strength." However, it is also cited by our detractors to denigrate Jews, Judaism, God, and all religion. The dialog begins with verse 7 of the chapter, as Abraham and his son Isaac ascend to the place where God has directed Abraham to offer up his beloved son as a Burnt Offering.

Isaac: My Father, here is the fire and here is the wood; but where is the lamb for the offering?

Abraham: That is a deep question, my Son. A very deep question!

I: And what is the answer, my Father?

A: *The Lord will see to the lamb for His Offering, my Son.*

I: That is a very deep answer, my Father!

A: Why do you think so?

I: Because it is the kind of answer that comes from the Lord, and not from the world.

A: How so, my Son?

I: Wood, we should have found; fire, we could have made. God must have said something about the lamb.

A: And so He has.

I: Did God also tell you to bring the fire and the wood?

A: No. That was my own idea.

I: And you have the knife — I saw you whet it. Yet something is troubling you. Should we perhaps have brought stones for the altar?

A: And how many stones from Gerar should we bring up to desecrate Moriah? Would that your limbs were strong enough for three days' pulling such a cart! We had cleansed this land of much impurity!

I: Yet something is weighing on you like a ton of stones! Why do you not share your thoughts with me and lighten your burden?

A: I am weighing in my mind whether it is right to deprive an animal of its life in order to make a Burnt Offering to God.

I: Is that not a heavy question to be asking at this very moment?

A: Why do you think it heavy, my Son?

I: Did not Cain ask the same question when he and Abel were building an altar to God?

A: Cain's sin lay in his answer, not in his question.

I: But what makes you ponder this question now, since God's request will moot your answer, whatever it may be?

A: Not long before you were by the Grace of God conceived, I stood before Sodom to ask God whether the guilty should not be redeemed for the sake of the guiltless. Today I question whether it is right to sacrifice the guiltless for the sake of the guilty.

I: But did God not ask for a Burnt Offering? Surely it is not a Guilt Offering that He demanded of you!

A: My question is a universal one. Sin exists in the world, but the remedy is Repentance. Repentance is Regret, Resolve and Atonement. Atonement is through suffering. But suffering draws us inward into ourselves; therefore, God, in His great wisdom and mercy, gave us a way to draw us out through sacrifice. If it is a sin to sacrifice an animal, how shall we atone for it?

I: What did God answer when you stood before Sodom?

A: You know the story, my Son: I would have argued to save even one innocent, but God would not hear me beyond ten. And ten could not be found. Now that God has commanded me to prepare a Burnt Offering, I am reminded that no living being goes willingly to the slaughter!

I: But Father, will a dog not sacrifice its life in order to save its master? A camel once trod on a snake that crept behind me!

A: Ah? This I did not know! When did that happen?

I: I was still a small boy. I did not tell you or Mama, as I did not want to upset you.

A: It is good that you did not tell Mama; but you should not hide such things from me! What happened?

I: The camel died, but the snake died first.

A: I remember that camel! She was devoted to you. But that is not what I mean by sacrifice.

I: I know, Father. A dog will act unthinkingly to protect its master. So, it seems, will a camel.

A: A father, too, will without thought protect his child, whatever the cost.

I: And the child, when big enough, will do the same for his father.

A: Yes, all that is true. It is an inner movement born of love. There is no time or need to reflect.

I: And if there were time?

A: You know that even given time to consider the outcome, I would not hesitate for a moment . . .

I: I know, Father! But what about an animal? If given time to reflect, would a dog risk its life to save its master?

A: Your camel knew what death lies coiled within a snake. Nevertheless, she chose to protect you.

I: Yes. That is love. But it is like the love of a camel for her calves, a love implanted by God, like a *Mitzvah*, a Commandment. Even a wild ram will stand against a lion to protect its young.

A: So a ram can do *Mitzvos*?

I: Why not, Father? Does it not perform the *Mitzvah* of *P'ru Ur'vu* — "Be fruitful and multiply?" But the *Mitzvah* of Burnt Offering it cannot do.

A: And why is that?

I: Because to make of itself an offering to God goes against the will-to-survive which He implanted in it.

A: But so does the duty to protect one's children.

I: Does it, Father? Surely, that duty is part of *P'ru Ur'vu*! But God did not give the ram a Commandment to jump onto the altar and stretch out its neck.

A: Nor, to my knowledge, has a sheep or a goat ever jumped into the fire in order to raise a savory smoke. But why would God give such a Commandment? Where is the benefit to the ram? What would motivate the ram to sacrifice its life to God Who gave it life?

I: Gratitude?

A: And if I give you a gold necklace, do you thank me by giving it back to me?

I: No. Of course not! It would be an impudent and unthankful gesture! And yet, do we not make Thank Offerings from the flocks which God has bestowed on us?

A: To express our gratitude for the increase thereof, lest we credit ourselves for the success of our labor. Besides, how do you know that a sheep feels gratitude?

I: I know that when I feed a lamb in the pen, it nuzzles my hand. So if it feels thankful to me in its pen, will it not feel thankful to God in the field?

A: Whether in the field or in the pen, does a lamb know that it is really God Who feeds it?

I: You are right, Father! I do not know what a lamb knows or does not know.

A: Neither do I, my Son. In any case, the lamb will not be so thankful that it will gladly give up its life on the altar.

I: Nor is it an offering to God when an animal sacrifices its life for its young. We have established that. But a son of Adam is able to feel gratitude, is he not, Father?

A: One would hope so, my Son.

I: Well then, if a man climbed up on the altar and cut through his own gullet as a Thank Offering to God, would God accept it?

A: Of course not! Did we not just agree that it would be a terrible affront? It is forbidden! It would be a sin and a crime!

I: But say he did it out of an excess of guilt and remorse.

A: Such an act is forbidden by the Laws of Noah. It is self-murder.

I: Agreed. But don't our neighbors, the Philistines, practice human sacrifice?

A: Yes, they do. And so do many other Nations. It is idolatry. They say they do it to appease the anger of their gods.

I: Why would their gods be angry, if not for such abominations?

A: Their gods are not angry. Their gods are of the same stone with which they build their sacrificial altars. If a stone could harbor anger, it would be for this very abuse which they endure. It is God Who sends them their troubles, as He sends us ours.

I: But do we sacrifice a lamb or a ram to appease God's anger?

A: Sometimes. But God is slow to anger. Mostly, we sacrifice to express repentance or thanks. Sometimes to seal a covenant or sweeten a plea. Always to express love and fear of Him.

I: And how does slaughtering a ram, for example, express those things?

A: By substitution: "Father in Heaven, You have given me Life! My life is the most precious thing I possess. I would give You what is most precious to me." But, once again: did we not agree that it would be effrontery to return a precious gift in thanks for that very gift?

I: We did.

A: And that it would be contrary to the Law?

I: Yes, Father.

A: And if, God forbid! a man should forfeit his life through sin, will death correct him?

I: His sentence may correct him, but his execution will not.

A: So the ram's life is given in exchange for our own. Did God not give the sons of Adam dominion over all the animals? He has also endowed us with a reverence for all life—a portion of His compassion. The ram's life is precious to me also. When I offer the ram as a Burnt Offering, a part of my life is consumed with it. My heart goes out to it, as we say, and the pain I feel over its sacrifice sharpens my gratitude for my own life and all life, and for the food I eat that keeps me alive. For surely, if I decline to slaughter the ram on God's altar, must I not also demur to slaughter it for my table?

I: Yes, I agree that it would be impudence to do otherwise. But Father, is your compassion a sufficient price to pay for the life of the ram?

A: That is the very question I have been meditating for the past three days.

I: And have you found an answer?

A: The best that I have found, my Son, is that if my Offering draws me out of myself, teaches me to feel the suffering of others, and inspires me to repair the wrongs I have done and to raise the level on which I deal with God and the world, then yes, perhaps I am justified in taking the ram's life—as long as it is done correctly, with the prescribed blessings, the proper intent, and according to the laws of humane slaughter.

I: Well, then the Philistines must feel love and repentance more deeply than we, Father, must they not?

A: Why?

I: Because to slaughter a human being must arouse in them more compassion than to slaughter an animal.

A: Must it? An idol worshipper's sensibilities are very different from ours. Besides, the victims they sacrifice are often criminals or captives taken in war, for whom they feel even less compassion than for an animal!

I: Criminals or captives . . . often, but not always?

A: No. They occasionally sacrifice their own children, God have mercy!

I: To please their gods of stone?

A: So they claim to believe. Horrifying, but true.

I: And if they sacrificed their children to the One True God?

A: It would be all the more repulsive.

I: What if one of our own did it?

A: A Hebrew? God forbid! It would be an odious transgression, a desecration of God's name, would it not? Has He not prohibited it among the Seven Laws?

I: But the Seven Laws are for the instruction of the children of Adam. Does God Himself not take life away from animals and men when it pleases Him to do so?

A: Yes, my Son, but that does not count as a sacrifice. God does not sacrifice to Himself!

I: But if God commanded a man to do it, then wouldn't the man be acting as God's agent?

A: So it would seem.

I: Thus removing from the man both the blame for the transgression and the merit of the offering?

A: That is interesting. I must think about that. So are you suggesting that an offering may not be genuine if performed at God's behest?

I: How can it be genuine if the intent is God's and not the man's?

A: But have we not just seen that man is the only creature who can sacrifice to God? In our Teachings, all that is required in the way of intent is that the one who offers should mean to carry out God's will as conveyed through His Laws or as commanded to His Servants. But to this one can add that if, in order to carry out God's will, the man must suppress his own will, then it becomes a true sacrifice. Now tell me, my Son: how did we arrive at human sacrifice from a simple question about the absence of a lamb?

I: Did you not say, my Father, that it was a deep question?

A: I did, my Son. And I answered that God would see to the lamb.

I: Indeed. For we have brought wood and fire, but no lamb for the offering. Wood we should have found. Fire we could have made. Father, you would not deceive me by bringing the lamb, but you have brought wood and fire lest your Offering turn tail and run while you are busy chopping wood and kindling fire!

A: No, my Son, no! It is simply that I could not find words to tell you what God has commanded me to do. The wood and the fire have spoken for me.

I: But why, Father? Why has God put this burden upon you? Have I sinned, Father? Have I brought this misfortune upon us with some inadvertent transgression?

A: God forbid, my Son! On the contrary, God has surely chosen you for your sinless, unblemished Soul and body, in which He delights.

I: I could have hoped to delight Him more with my life than with my death!

A: So could I, my Son! But since God has commanded it, I must suppress my own will and my love, and obey. And so must you, my son.

I: Has God offered no reason, no explanation?

A: Who should ask God to explain His reasons? If God will offer me a reason, I will share it with you.

I: I cannot imagine that God's reasons will make this Command easier for you or me to obey. Can you, Father?

A: No, my Son, I cannot.

I: Then it must be a test. God is surely testing your loyalty.

A: And yours.

I: Then once you have proven your loyalty, God will surely retract His Command. Tell me, Father: is it true what they say about Nimrod, how he threw you into a red-hot furnace?

A: I have no personal recollection of it, only a vague memory of being happy beyond words, as though I were in the presence of God. They told me, after I awoke, that when the stoker opened the furnace, they found me smiling and speechless amid the ashes. They say this happened after Nimrod ordered me to bow down to his idols on pain of being burnt alive. But I would not have considered that a test. What choice did I have? It is the Law! Any one of my students would have done the same to sanctify God's Name. But such a thing is neither a sacrifice nor a test. Now, however, I must perform this new act, which the Law abhors, to prove my personal loyalty to God.

I: Perhaps if you had been less eager to honor the Law, the Holy One would not have placed this test upon you; for He certainly knows how terrible it is for you. God will surely relent once you say the Blessing.

A: You know very well that once I say the Blessing, I must complete the act. To forestall the act would be to take God's Name in vain.

I: But if the idolators hear that a Servant of God has done as they do, will they not all the more regard such acts as laudable? Can it be God's intent to encourage their crimes? Father, it must be a test! God will surely relent as soon as you take the knife into your hand!

A: My Son! How can we pass this test if we believe that it is only a test? God probes the depths of every heart and soul and knows our every thought. This knot I am unable to untie. How can I complete this Offering with the proper intent?

I: Then let me tell you, Father, that I hope to lie upon the altar as blissfully as you lay in Nimrod's furnace. Indeed, I am happy to have been chosen for this Offering, and I trust that you will complete the act with a joyful heart, untainted by grief or regret or guilt of any kind.

A: But did we not establish a while ago that the essence of sacrifice is to quicken repentance and love? How can I rejoice in carrying out an act over which I am destined to grieve for the rest of my life? Besides, if I were to enjoy performing this *Mitzvah*, what kind of a test would it be? And I, what kind of man, what kind of father would I be?

I: It is indeed a hard knot! How is one to perform with a joyful heart an act whose very purpose and consequence are to break it?

A: It seems this is something I must still learn. For although I have always rejoiced to honor God's Commandments, I can see no joy in this. Yet I know with certainty that I shall greatly mourn unto my grave.

I: And not you alone! How will you break the news to Mama?

A: Is one way better than another? How can I inflict this suffering on my beloved Sarah? I shall never be able to face her again.

I: And if God relents?

A: Then you must run to Mama as fast as you can! Let her see before she hears! As for me, what a ransom for your dear life! Henceforth, my Sarah will never again look upon me without bitterness in her heart. For, like you, she will know as soon she hears we went up without the animal.

I: My Father, will Mama turn against God?

A: No! Never!

I: Then how should Mama turn against you?

A: Women are different, my son. God was careful to let Mama overhear when He blessed her to bear a son. But He was careful to hide from her what He has asked me to do with her baby. Have you ever seen a lioness defend her young?

I: Then, Father, you must not neglect to bind my hands and feet, lest the Spirit within me turn into a lioness as you approach with the knife.

A: You have spoken wisely, my Son!

I: And yet, I am greatly troubled. For whatever joy or grief you may find in the performance of this *Mitzvah*, your reward for accomplishing it promises to be the cruelest punishment. Surely this contradicts everything you have taught?

A: God forbid! What have I been teaching for the last 100 years? Only Good can come from the performance of a *Mitzvah*! The harder it is to perform, the greater the Good that must come from it!

I: Then is it not true, that a very great Good must come from what we are about to do?

A: You are right, my Son! Something exceedingly Great and Good beyond measure!

I: Then let us build our altar with joyful hearts and complete trust in God.

A: Amen! May it be so! Now, let us start with that heavy stone over there . . .

I: Look Father! It is not heavy. It is not heavy at all!

* * *

Requiem for a Rooster (Dec. 8-17, 2020)

Last May, in the village of Vinzieux, France, a man shot and impaled his neighbor's rooster. The owner sued the shooter and circulated a petition demanding justice. More than 100,000 people signed it! This is a classically French phenomenon.

To poets, the rooster symbolizes the three pillars of democracy: Vigilance, Truth and Freedom of Speech. To the French, a people of poetry and democratic ideals, the rooster also symbolizes France herself, particularly because the word "gallus" (the Latin word for "rooster" and its scientific name) means "inhabitant of Gaul"—in other words, the people of France!

My poem begins with a free translation of the petitioner's resounding verses:

Alors, qui sera la prochaine victime:
Le chant des tourterelles,
La moisson du blé,
Les tomates qui poussent,
Le braiment de l'âne,
Le son de nos clochers
Ou la mise en pâturage de nos vaches?

      — Sebastien Verney, Vinzieux, France

Who will be the next to fall?
The chirring of the turtle doves?
the harvesting of summer wheat?
Tomatoes burgeoning on the vine?
The donkey's braying hee-haw hee-haw?
The ringing of our tower bells?
The putting out to pasture of our cows?

Long live your chirring turtle doves
the summer harvests of your wheat
the ripening tomatoes on your vine
the donkey practising his raucous line
the church bells ringing the passing hours
and calling to the faithful from your towers;
long live the grazing of your lowing herds,
and the putting out to pasture of your words!

Marcel, Marcel, named for a mime!
Martyr and Patriot, poet sublime,
long live your memory, valiant bird!
Long may your voice of brass be heard!
Wake up the barnyard with your rhyme!

Raise hell, Marcel, raise bloody hell!
Chante-le depuis ton poullaier dans le ciel!
declaim it from your hen house in the sky!
Are we to follow and not reason why?
Raise hue and cry old cockerel!
Cry Justice, old cockadoodle sentinel!
Cry Liberty throughout the land!
Arouse the people to the task at hand!
Cry *Liberté! Egalité! Fraternité!*
Et n'oublions pas l'Humanité!
Remind us — may we never forget
the heroic deeds of gallant Lafayette
who penned, along with Jefferson
Les Droits de l'Homme et du Citoyen!
Cry *Vive la Résistance!* Cry *Vive la Différence!*
Car il s'agit même de notre existence!

Workers and citizens, arise! Unite!
Jump out of bed, turn on the light!
Lace up your boots! Prepare to fight!
Raise your voice to the very heights!
Defend your Constitution and your Bill of Rights!
The College-Quarter Communists,
revanchists and revisionists,
through subterfuge and grosselüge,
have played their hand, now overreach
to quash your right to arms and speech,
and, with unvetted ballots round your throat,
constrict the People's franchise — yes! your right to vote! —
prisons releasing prisoners to make room,
while new prisons are building! And for whom?

Go sing it loud and clear, Marcel!
Wake up! Wake up! Don't drink this cup —
poisoned with kitchmarxian swill and slop!
Once more unto the breach pell-mell!
The fox is in the chicken coop,
the farmer's in the dell!

Shall I bid you sleep peacefully, Marcel?
Shall I wish you rest peacefully, Marcel?
No rest, no sleep, no peace, for you, Marcel . . .
till the Conspiracy wake up in hell!

Letter to Baudelaire (Dec. 20-23, 2020)

I don't write letters to dead poets much.
Not since I mailed one to Hermann Hesse
believing him alive. The letter was returned
"Deceased." He must have passed
while I was filling and refilling my pen.
I wonder what I wrote to him at last.

    But I can't help thinking about them. Can you?
Has it happened to you that someone
you've been thinking about intensely
suddenly pops up — "makes himself alive,"
as the Italians say, who make an art
of living in the distant past?

    But writing to you, dear Poet,
is like speaking to the living.
Or talking to the flowers.
So why not? Wet lips, *cul sec*!
You, too, took refuge in something,
though, truth be told, your solitary
was a far cry from mine.
A far cry, Paris, for all your gripes!
I wouldn't mind a puff right now —
if you could share a pinch.

    I just wanted to propose —
no, not a toast, but if I might suggest —
it's not so much that poets can't walk —
they get along alright! It's just —
you know, like Thoreau said —
the world heeds a different drummer,
dances to a different tune?
Put *that* in your pipe and smoke it!
I know. You did. The bowl still glows.

    Except that now, it seems
we're all of us in the same parade
single file and far apart
like at the supermart!
Which is nothing new, really, is it?

Always the proverbial six feet!
Six feet asunder or six feet under!
How long between the lightning and the thunder?
How long until the Government Inspector?

   How long until your next visit?
As for me, I'm waiting for my walking papers, *Ha ha!*
No need to reply, *cher Maître.* No need to add
to what you wrote. You ask, "*Comment ça va?*"
Ça marche, ça marche . . .

A Quarrel with the Moon (Dec. 24-26, 2020)
Baudelaire, "*La lune offensée*"

Too many poet-translators have read this sonnet as treating of love and sex! Larousse, litcrit, and the text itself are quite clear: The poet rails against the ostentatious hypocrisy of his times and the meretricious pursuit of superficial splendor. He decries the ruinous neglect of the cultural and urban landscape which formed him from infancy. Overcome with indignation and frustration, he vents his rage against the moon for her perpetual, impassive and ineffectual orbiting of the disarray. The moon, rightly offended, replies with a terrible insult. However, the poet has merely placed his own judgement in her mouth: It is his own maternal city, the Paris of an "impoverished century," that merits castigation, not the blameless moon!

O Moon, whom modestly our forebears would entreat:
from high the azure lands, where like serail of fire
the stars encircle you, arranging their attire,
my old, dear Cynthia, lamp of our bygone retreat,

d'you see the lovers in their prosperous shame reclining,
see from their sleeping mouths the freshly enameled smirk?
the poet banging his head in vain against his work?
beneath neglected lawns the coupled snakes entwining?

And yellow-gowned and masqued, with surreptitious gait
you still, from dusk to daybreak, as of yore, go creeping
to kiss the wizened charms of old Endymion sleeping?

"Your mother I see, Child of a century impov'rished,
lurching to her mirror, of years with heavy weight
to powder-puff with guile the breast where you were nourished!"

Blessing (December 14, *Motzoei Shabbos*, 2019)

Hand stencil paintings in caves in Spain, Argentina (Cueva de las Manos), and Sulawesi (Celebes) Island in the Malay Archipelago have recently been re-dated to circa 40–to–60 thousand years ago (tens of thousands of years older than previously thought), thanks to a new method of dating calcium deposits ("popcorn") formed over portions of the artwork. The new chronology is considered more accurate than that obtained by traditional carbon-14 dating because the decay of uranium particles in the "popcorn" can be measured with much higher precision than the radioactive carbon contained in the pigments. As if this new chronology were not enough, it also raises the possibility that some of the paintings were done by our immediate human predecessors, Homo neanderthalensis. *Reading about this on Erev Shabbos, I was so moved that I could hardly think about anything else until the departure of* Shabbos, *when I wrote the following:*

I've seen so many careless arrows fly,
I paint myself all over a bright red
with something my woman uses for dye
that I find hidden in her potting shed.

But not to taint my food before they dry,
I lay my hands against the wall instead
and spray the back of each alternately
keeping the palms pressed flat with fingers spread.

When I am done, I laugh. The wife asks why.
I answer her, not seeing trouble ahead,
"Now, when I'm gone, no need for you to cry —
you'll see me wave wherever you turn your head!".

She yells at me, "You fool! I know this stuff!
A hundred years, you'll never get it off!"

EXPLICIT LIBER POIKILOPAIDIA

TABLE OF POEMS

Patapon	13
Let Darkness Fall	14
Still Reasoning with Me (Petrarca)	14
Orpheus	15
Sea Change	15
Musa Mea	16
In Defense of Humanism	16
Argos	17
Before a Japanese Print	17
Dolce Stil Novo	18
Thanksgiving	18
Bucephalus	19
To the Poet Who Said that Sappho . . .	19
To the Same, Calling Sappho "Strident"	20
Ode to Aphrodite (Sappho)	21
Asylum	22
On Reading Eliot's Introduction to Pound	23
Film Criticism	23
Snails and Ships	23
Indovinello	24
Life's Art	24
Water Music	24
Far Lights	24
Dialog Before a Tomb at Cesri	25
Meeting	25
Speculation	26
A New Noah	27
Archipelago	27
Si Fossi Foco (Cecco Angiolieri)	28
Fool's Prayer	28
To Myself (after Guido Cavalcanti)	29
Letter to Miss Lonely Hearts	29
To a Blonde	30
The Wind & the Soap Bubble	31
Choreography for a Dream	33
Poikilopaidia	35
Dedication	36

Table of Contents	36
Manifesto	37
The Lion's Share	37
To a Portrait of Sheryl	38
Paolo's Reproach (Paolo Montalbini)	38
Song Without Words	39
Fog (Hermann Hesse)	41
Aias (Vincenzo Cardarelli)	41
DRN: Hymn to Venus and Proem (Lucretius)	43
Comic Strip, Fikellura Style	51
Golgotha	51
Appendix	52
Algernon	52
Old Black Man at the Pet Store	53
Exercise	54
BLDGS	54
Bead Game	55
Pygmalion	56
Mit Diesem Kuss	57
Poetry My Ars	59
A Silvia (Leopardi)	68
On the Interpretation of Beethoven . . .	70
Each in His Own Way	73
The Question	73
Apologia	77
Dim Star	78
The Legacy	78
Portent	79
Torso (Rilke)	80
The Apple Garden (Rilke)	80
He Who Has Art	82
March 12, 1989	82
Allegory	83
Prophecy (Tommaso Campanella)	83
Syllogism	84
Rebuttal	84
The Book (after Giovanni Pascoli)	85

First in thought	86
Wrestler's Prayer	87
A Prayer	87
Teshuvah:	88
1 Oniah:	88
2 Day & Night	89
3 The Heart Knows	90
4 Believe it or Not	91
5 Deposition	91
The Other Side:	92
Sweet Rice:	93
To Ben Before His Journey	93
Those Dancin' Feet	94
Politician	94
Dante in Disneyland: Canto VII	95
The Mocking Bird	101
To a Literary Agent	101
Basket Case	104
At the Barber Shop	104
Pseudo - Philodemi Poenitentia	106
Chinese Interlude:	108
1 Correspondence	108
2 Tonight the Moon	109
3 Those Were Not Petals (Xi Murong)	109
4 Tonight You Are the Moon (Xi Murong?)	109
5 There Are No Secrets	110
6 Moon Festival	110
7. Ideogram	111
8. Asian Lilies	111
A Green Haze	111
Fire Break	112
Neanderthal	112
Adolescence (Vincenzo Cardarelli)	113
That Coltish Look	114
The True Story of the Lobster & the Octopus	115
Francesca e Paolo (Dante's *Inferno*, Canto V)	119
Driving to Vegas	124

A Passing Thought	124
To the Abstainers	124
A Sense of Loss	128
The Turtle's Complaint	128
Zen Pond	128
Breakfast News	129
Bogeys	130
The Color of Sky Before Snow	130
The Flowering Pear	131
The Rocking Chair	131
Fandango	132
The Voice in the Mirror	133
Some Thoughts on Superman	133
Ceci n'est pas	135
Memory as a Convex Mirror	136
The Gift	136
Complaint for Breach of Duty to Disclose	139
On Granados's "Quejas, o La Maja . . ."	140
Answering my Mother's Question	140
Mathematics and Madness	142
Russell's Teapot	143
I Love the Spider (after Victor Hugo)	145
What the Torah Doesn't Tell us	146
Thoughts from a Leather Couch	146
Q & A	147
Dead or Alive	149
Reprieve	150
Ravens & Rooklets	151
Dord	151
Reality Check	153
The Ant and the Lion	153
Rainbow Witness	153
The Lens Grinder	154
Driving up the Mountain in a Thick Fog	155
Forelius Pusillus	156
How Are You?	159
La Bellissima Biondina	159

A Woman You Have Loved	160
The Ancestry of Flowers	160
Echein kai ouk Echein	162
A Bee in Switzerland	163
Black Coffee Blues	163
A Matter of Perspective	164
Kites	164
The Institute of Anguish	164
A Falling Leaf	165
Charlie's Angel	170
Analysis: The Blues	172
Phonecall	173
Time Capsule	174
Birdwatching	175
That Fleeting Shade of Green	175
Korach	176
Resumé	177
Shortcuts	178
The Moon Up Close	179
How Old Am I Now?	180
Spinoza's Birds	180
Protest	183
A Parable	183
Windsock	184
Akila's Howl	184
My Russian Novel	185
The Vicar	188
The Cloud	189
A Bagel's Lament	189
Snapshot	191
Laughing Buddha	192
The Silent Teapot	197
The Pyromane: On Rereading Frost	197
The Safety Pin	198
Janus or Sejanus	199
Book Case	200
Androcles	200

The Painted Lady	200
A Tale of Two Cities	201
Schubert's Fantasy	204
Visit	205
Translation of a Dali Painting	206
At the Sign of the Swan	206
A Brief Note on Mallarmé & George	219
The Music Box	223
Freedom and Flannel Trousers	223
Luciole	223
Girasole	224
Around the Corner	226
Dialog of Abraham & Isaac	227
Requiem for a Rooster	238
Letter to Baudelaire	240
A Quarrel with the Moon (Baudelaire)	241
Blessing	**242**

OTHER WORKS BY PETER GIMPEL

Thinking Back The River Runs Uphill (a polymorphic novel)

The Carnevalis of Eusebius Asch (a polymorphic novel)

Professor Gansa's Dream, or Science as a Naked Lightbulb:
a parable in 75 "stanzos" comprising
a Jewish reply to Carl Sagan's
Demon-Haunted World: Science as a Candle in the Dark
(with eleven visualizations by Gerry McGuinness)

Twilight with Halfmoon Rising
(selected poems — incorporated in this volume)

Essays & Articles published on the author's Literary Blog
at www.redheiferpress.com

ABOUT RED HEIFER PRESS

Red Heifer Press is a small, independent publishing company dedicated to the publishing of literary fiction, poetry, documentary memoirs (especially of Holocaust Survivors), Belles Lettres, Torah/Judaica, and scholarship in the Humanities, the Sciences, and Jurisprudence. We seek original, quality work out of the mainstream.

Red Heifer Press also provides editorial services to writers in the above-listed categories. Our services include typing, transcribing, translation (French, German, Italian) to ghostwriting, book development, critiquing, formatting, design, and consulting.

For further information, please visit www.redheiferpress.com
Telephone: 661.822.3438
Email: editor@redheiferpress.com

Typeset in Goudy Old Style

Notes

Notes

www.ingramcontent.com/pod-product-compliance
Lightning Source LLC
Chambersburg PA
CBHW032032290426
44110CB00012B/768